BBC

DOCTOR WHO

THE TENTH DOCTOR

VOL 7: WAR OF GODS

"One of the best stories to be told via the comic book medium."
SNAP POW

"This book truly feels like a lost episode of the RTD era of *Doctor Who*."
MY GEEKY GEEKY WAYS

"Nick Abadzis crafts yet another compelling story!"
FANDOM POST

"The best of Titan Comics' slate of *Doctor Who* comics."
GIANT FREAKING ROBOT

"Abadzis does a wonderful job of drawing us in and weaving the world around us..."
GEEK GIRL PROJECT

"Perfectly captures the spirit of *Doctor Who*!"
KABOOOOOM!

"Writer Nick Abadzis, along with the smooth and engaging art by Giorgia Sposito, shows that traveling with the Doctor isn't just all alien planets and daring escapes."
NEWSARAMA

"Wonderfully written and flows perfectly!"
POP CULTURE BANDIT

"*Doctor Who* fans are well-served."
SOUNDS ON SIGHT

"The *Doctor Who* comic fans have always deserved."
BLOODY DISGUSTING

"The Tenth Doctor will spirit you away with some cool horns, some hot jazz, and some superlative storytelling from four players at the top of their game."
WARPED FACTOR

TITAN COMICS

COLLECTION EDITOR
Jessica Burton

SENIOR COMICS EDITOR
Andrew James

ASSISTANT EDITORS
Amoona Saohin

COLLECTION DESIGNER
Andrew Leung

TITAN COMICS EDITORIAL
Tom Williams, Lauren McPhee

PRODUCTION SUPERVISOR
Maria Pearson

PRODUCTION CONTROLLER
Peter James

SENIOR PRODUCTION CONTROLLER
Jackie Flook

ART DIRECTOR
Oz Browne

SENIOR SALES MANAGER
Steve Tothill

PRESS OFFICER
Will O'Mullane

COMICS BRAND MANAGER
Chris Thompson

ADS & MARKETING ASSISTANT
Tom Miller

DIRECT SALES & MARKETING MANAGER
Ricky Claydon

COMMERCIAL MANAGER
Michelle Fairlamb

HEAD OF RIGHTS
Jenny Boyce

PUBLISHING MANAGER
Darryl Tothill

PUBLISHING DIRECTOR
Chris Teather

OPERATIONS DIRECTOR
Leigh Baulch

EXECUTIVE DIRECTOR
Vivian Cheung

PUBLISHER
Nick Landau

For rights information contact Jenny Boyce
jenny.boyce@titanemail.com

Special thanks to Steven Moffat, Brian Minchin, Mandy Thwaites, Matt Nicholls, James Dudley, Edward Russell, Derek Ritchie, Scott Handcock, Kirsty Mullan, Kate Bush, Julia Nocciolino and Ed Casey for their invaluable assistance.

BBC WORLDWIDE

DIRECTOR OF EDITORIAL GOVERNANCE
Nicholas Brett

DIRECTOR OF CONSUMER PRODUCTS AND PUBLISHIN
Andrew Moultrie

HEAD OF UK PUBLISHING
Chris Kerwin

PUBLISHER
Mandy Thwaites

PUBLISHING CO-ORDINATOR
Eva Abramik

DOCTOR WHO: THE TENTH DOCTOR VOL 7: WAR OF GODS
HB ISBN: 9781785860867
SB ISBN: 9781785860904
Published by Titan Comics, a division of Titan Publishing Group, Ltd. 144 Southwark Street, London, SE1 0UP.

A CIP catalogue record for this title is available from th British Library.
First edition: May 2017.

10 9 8 7 6 5 4 3 2 1

Printed in China.

www.titan-comics.com

BBC

DOCTOR WHO

THE TENTH DOCTOR

VOL 7: WAR OF GODS

WRITERS: NICK ABADZIS
& JAMES PEATY

ARTISTS: GIORGIA SPOSITO
& WARREN PLEECE

COLORISTS: ARIANNA FLOREAN
& HI-FI

LETTERS: RICHARD STARKINGS AND
COMICRAFT'S JIMMY BETANCOURT

THE DOCTOR

Last of the Time Lords of Gallifrey, the Tenth Doctor still hides his post-Time War guilt beneath a happy-go-lucky guise. Never cruel or cowardly, he champions the oppressed across time and space – but his last adventure has left him shaken.

GABBY GONZALEZ

Gabriella Gonzalez is a young would-be artist from Sunset Park, Brooklyn, New York, who is traveling the universe at the Tenth Doctor's side. Her youthful spirit and artistic eye are coupled to an adventurous and quick-witted mind!

CINDY WU

Gabby's fiercely loyal best frien now traveling with her in the TARDIS. She has earned her place ten times over, but even Cindy can still be surpised by what their adventures can throw at her!

PREVIOUSLY...

The Doctor, Gabby, and Cindy were summoned to the *Shining Horizon* to help Anubis with a project – ascending home through the Circle of Transcendence without destroying the Universe in the process! But things have not gone at all to plan. While searching for primordial spare parts on ancient Gallifrey, the Doctor and Cindy were ambushed by Aspects of the Time Sentinel, intent on throwing them into the Untempered Schism! Though they both escaped, the Doctor fears this may not be the last they see of Sentinel. Meanwhile, back on the *Shining Horizon*, Dorothy and Gabby are also in grave danger – Sutekh has risen again, in the body of his son!

When you've finished reading this collection, please email your thoughts to doctorwhocomic@titanemail.com

NO...

HE... I HAVE TO--
DOROTHY, WAIT...

SOME MEASURE OF RESTORATION...
THE RECOVERY PLAN IS SUCCESSFULLY INITIATED.
MASTER?

DEED. I AM UR MASTER. I WILL DO MY BIDDING.
SENSORS DETECT ANOMALOUS BRAINWAVE PATTERNS.
MASTER, I WILL HAVE THE MEDICAL SERVITORS--

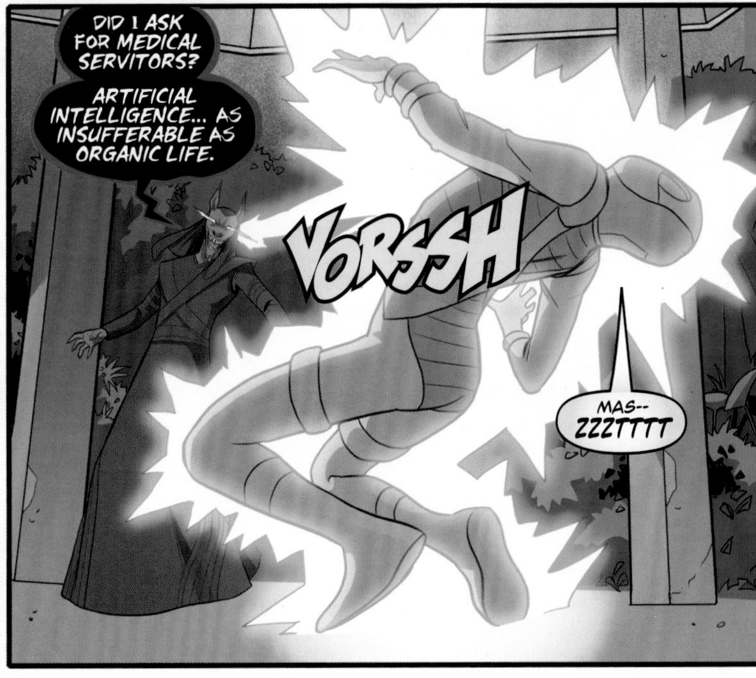
DID I ASK FOR MEDICAL SERVITORS?
ARTIFICIAL INTELLIGENCE... AS INSUFFERABLE AS ORGANIC LIFE.
VORSSH
MAS-- ZZZTTTT

NO. HE... HE WOULDN'T DO THAT. THE SEEKER WAS HIS ONLY COMPANION FOR MILLENNIA...
HEAR WHAT THE SEEKER SAID? HE'S NOT IN HIS RIGHT MIND...

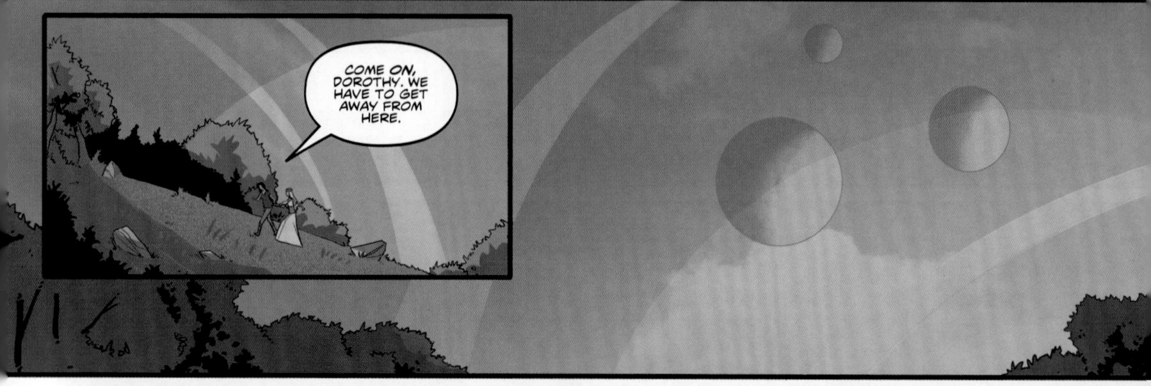
COME ON, DOROTHY. WE HAVE TO GET AWAY FROM HERE.

DID HE JUST KILL THE SEEKER?
NO, SHE'S THE SHIPBOARD A.I. SHE RUNS ALMOST EVERYTHING. HE DESTROYED ONE OF HER PHYSICAL VESSELS...
HER MAIN NEURAL NEXUS IS IN THE CENTRAL CORE.
RIGHT NOW, SHE'S PROBABLY AS CONFUSED AS I AM.

THEN WE HAVE TO TALK TO HER.

I CAN DO THAT FROM HERE...
SEEKER, WHY DID ANUBIS ATTACK YOU?
SISTER...
WOW.

IT WAS NOT ANUBIS! NOT ANUBIS!
HIS CONSCIOUSNESS HAS BEEN... SIDELINED, HIS BODY STOLEN.
I AM EXPERIENCING... MY SYSTEMS...
ALL PATHWAYS ARE UNDER ATTACK. POWER IS BEING DIVERTED...

I HAVE TO CONTACT THE DOCTOR.
BEWARE -- DAMPENING FIELD... TRANSMISSIONS CAN BE MONITORED... TRACED.
AS YET, I BELIEVE HE'S UNAWARE OF YOUR PRESENCE.
SISTER, WHO IS UNAWARE...?

SUTEKH.
BEWARE SUTEKH!
WORST CASE SCENARIO CONFIRMED.
THE -- THE GHOST OF SUTEKH? HE'S DEAD! ISN'T HE?

HE IS RETURNING. A FRAGMENT OF HIM IS ALREADY HERE. HIS CONSCIOUSNESS... IT ATTACKS ME...
I MUST ISOLATE CORE SYSTEMS.
WE CAN HELP! TELL US HOW.
SISTER, IT IS MY DUTY TO HELP YOU.
YOU WERE ONCE, IN ANOTHER INCARNATION, THE HAND OF SUTEKH. HE WILL TRY TO RECLAIM YOU.
THAT MUST NOT HAPPEN.

BEWARE SUTEKH!
DARK ANUBIS... UM... ANUBEKH DOWN THERE IS ON THE MOVE.
HE MUST BE GOING TO THE CENTRAL CORE.
MAYBE WE CAN HELP THE SEEKER IF WE GET THERE BEFORE HIM.
UM, IS THAT WISE? YOU HEARD WHAT SHE SAID...
IF IT IS SUTEKH'S CONSCIOUSNESS, IT DOESN'T KNOW WE'RE HERE... YET.
BETTER STAY HIDDEN, THEN, HADN'T WE?
AT LEAST, UNTIL THE DOCTOR GETS BACK.
YOU'RE RIGHT.
IT TOOK THE COMBINED POWER OF OVER SEVEN HUNDRED AND FORTY OSIRANS TO OVERCOME HIM LAST TIME.
BUT I KNOW ANUBIS IS ALMOST AS POWERFUL AS HIS FATHER WAS.
AND I WANT MY DOGFACE BACK. SO WE'RE GOING TO HELP HIM, HOWEVER WE CAN.
WHOA!
I DOUBT EVEN SUTEKH WOULD SURVIVE IF WE RAMMED THIS MOTHERSHIP DOWN THE THROAT OF THE NEAREST BLACK HOLE.
BUT IT'S OK HONEY.
WE WON'T LET IT COME TO THAT.
HURRY UP, DOCTOR.

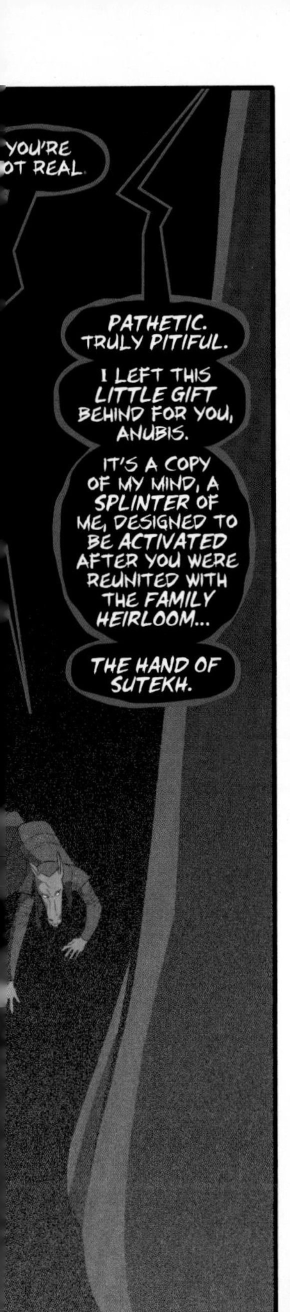

YOU'RE
OT REAL.
PATHETIC. TRULY PITIFUL.
I LEFT THIS LITTLE GIFT BEHIND FOR YOU, ANUBIS.
IT'S A COPY OF MY MIND, A SPLINTER OF ME, DESIGNED TO BE ACTIVATED AFTER YOU WERE REUNITED WITH THE FAMILY HEIRLOOM...
THE HAND OF SUTEKH.

I ASSURE YOU, I'M VERY REAL.
EVEN NOW, I AM TAKING OVER THE SHINING HORIZON, AS EASILY AS I POSSESSED YOUR BODY.
YOU'VE SPENT MONTHS SLOWLY HACKING INTO MY CONSCIOUSNESS...
I'VE BEEN UNKNOWINGLY FENDING YOU OFF FOR QUITE SOME TIME.
YOU HAD TO GROW STRONG ENOUGH TO ATTACK. YOU ARE SIMPLY A VIRUS.

A VIRUS THAT CAUSES YOU BLACKOUTS, THAT NOW FULLY INHABITS YOU... MIND, BODY AND SPIRIT.
I WILL CONSUME ALL THREE.
AAAAAAAAAA
VORSSH

YOU'RE WEAK. WHAT A DECREPIT BODY YOU HAVE, MY SON.
NO MATTER. SOON, I WILL RECOVER MY OWN... THE ORIGINAL SUTEKH, YOU MIGHT SAY.
... I KNOW EXACTLY HOW AND WHERE TO LOOK.
WE WILL BE WHOLE.
AND THEN WE WILL RENDER THE UNIVERSE UNTO DUST.

AMENTHES
ENERGY PRODUCTION FACILITY, OSIRAN REEFWORLDS COLONY.
SIX BILLION YEARS AGO.
Y'KNOW, I HAVE NEVER SEEN SUCH A WANTON DISPLAY OF FLIRTATION IN MY LIFE.
WAIT 'TIL I TELL GABBY THIS THE DOCTOR'S GO A THING FOR CA LADIES...
THAT SHOULD BE ENOUGH POWER TO REENERGIZE THE ENTIRE HABITAT.
UH-OH. I THOUGHT YOU SAID THESE OSIRANS WERE ON OUR SIDE NOW, DOCTOR...?
THEY ARE. SORT OF.

BIT USPICIOUS D NOT VERY PATIENT, THOUGH, OSIRANS.
NOT VERY GOOD AT *LENDING THINGS OUT*, EITHER.
WE -- WE'RE *STEALING* THE SCEPTER?
WELL, NO. WE'RE *BORROWING* IT AND IT'S FOR AN *EXCELLENT CAUSE...*
NOT ONLY IS IT HELPING *ANUBIS*, ONE OF THEIR OWN, IT'S FOR THE SAKE OF THE *FUTURE SAFETY OF THE COSMOS!*
POLICE PUBLIC CALL BO

BESIDES, WE'LL BRING IT BACK! *EVENTUALLY...*
THEY DON'T *KNOW* THAT.

YES, THEY *DO!* OR THEY *WILL* WHEN *SEKHMET TELLS* THEM...
DID YOU *GET* ALL THAT SEKHMET...?
DOCTOR, YOU BREAK A *LOT* OF RULES.
KTHUNN VWOORRRP

I *BEND* THEM. THERE'S ALWAYS A TEENSY-TINY BIT OF LEEWAY.
ESPECIALLY IF THERE'S SOME *TRUST* INVOLVED.
SEKHMET... I WOULD BE *HUGELY OBLIGED* IF YOU'D *SQUARE THIS* WITH *ATUM* AND THE *GUILD OF AGED SOULS...*
YOU GIVE ME *LITTLE CHOICE*, DOCTOR. YOU ARE *FORCING MY HAND AGAIN...*

OH, COME ON, DON'T BE LIKE THAT. ESPECIALLY NOT AFTER EVERYTHING WE'VE BEEN THROUGH TOGETHER...
WOULD YOU HAVE DEFEATED THE RACNOSS IMPERIUM AND THE CYCLOPIAN ALLIANCE WITHOUT MY HELP?
GO ON, ADMIT IT. YOU LIKE ME. I'M USEFUL.
I AM PROUD TO CALL YOU MY... MY FRIEND, DOCTOR.
THESE COLONY WORLDS OF PHAESTER OSIRIS WILL ALWAYS BE IN YOUR DEBT.
I'M GOING TO REGRET SAYING THIS...

GO, BEFORE THE GUILD KNOWS.
VWOORRRP
VWOORRRP
THANK YOU, SEKHMET! YOU'RE THE MOST FLEXIBLE OSIRAN I EVER MET!
FARE THEE WELL, TIME TRAVELERS. LOOK AFTER ALL OUR FUTURE INTERESTS.
UNTIL NEXT TIME.
"...THE STORY CONTINUES IN ANCIENT OSIRIS II - THE PURRING."

CRITICAL SYSTEM PATHWAYS DISENGAGED.
I'VE HELPED THE SEEKER PROTECT SOME IMPORTANT STUFF. SHE'LL PLAY ALONG.
LIFE SUPPORT SYSTEMS ARE RUNNING, BUT MOST OF THE POWER'S BEING DIVERTED AND I CAN'T FIGURE OUT WHERE TO.
DOROTHY, WE HAVE TO GO, *NOW*. ANUBEKH'S COMING.

WE CAN GET OUT THIS W--
HE'S TAKEN OVER THE *SERVITORS* TOO. *HIDE*.

SEEKER, YOU ARE UNABLE TO DENY THE *VERACITY* OF THIS *BIO-DATA PRINT*. RECOGNIZE MY AUTHORITY.
RECOGNIZED. BRAIN PATTERNS ANOMOLOUS--
OVERRIDE. CODE HORUS EPSIMECH AMON AKHTMU.
ACKNOWLEDGE NEW CO-ORDINATES AND INSTRUCTIONS.
CODE *ACCEPTED*. NEW PURPOSES *ACKNOWLEDGED*.

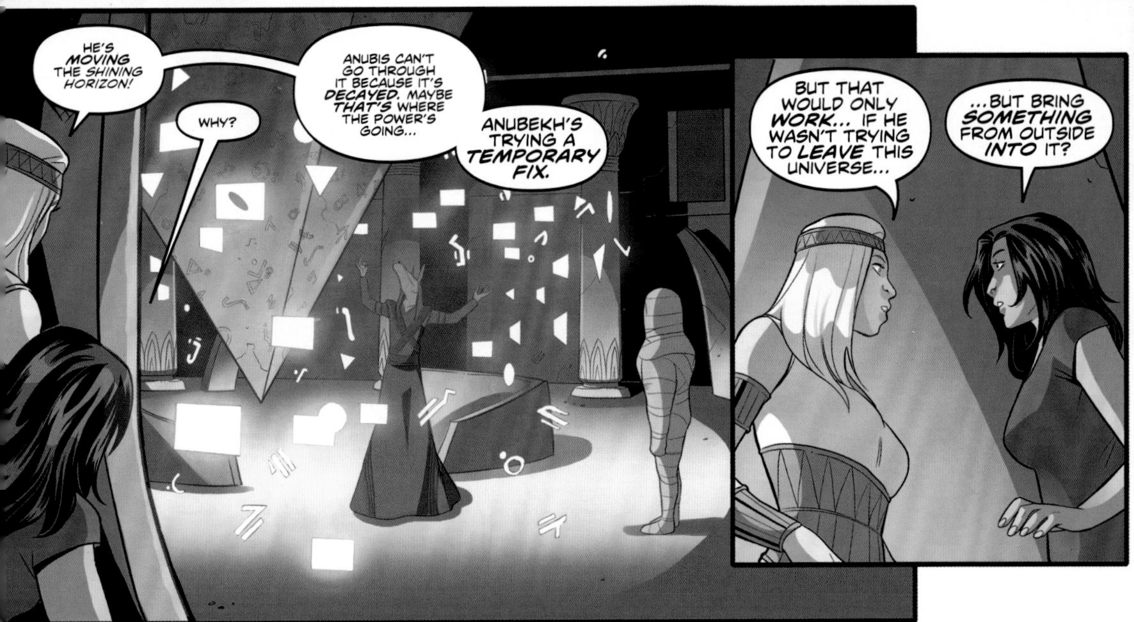
HE'S *MOVING* THE *SHINING HORIZON*!
WHY?
ANUBIS CAN'T GO THROUGH IT BECAUSE IT'S *DECAYED*. MAYBE *THAT'S* WHERE THE POWER'S GOING...
ANUBEKH'S TRYING A *TEMPORARY FIX*.
BUT THAT WOULD ONLY *WORK*... IF HE WASN'T TRYING TO *LEAVE* THIS UNIVERSE...
...BUT BRING *SOMETHING* FROM OUTSIDE *INTO* IT?

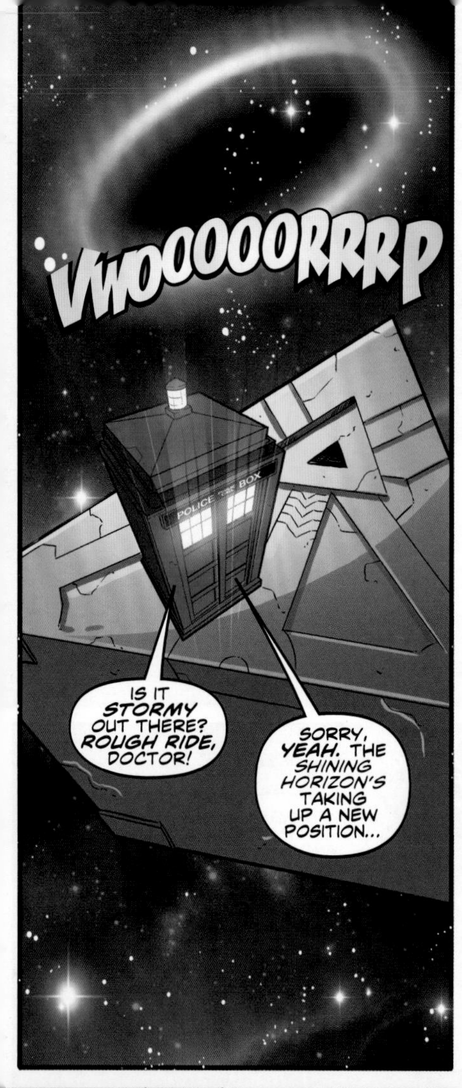
VWOOOOORRRP
IS IT STORMY OUT THERE? ROUGH RIDE, DOCTOR!
SORRY, YEAH. THE SHINING HORIZON'S TAKING UP A NEW POSITION...
POLICE BOX

ANUBIS IS IMPATIENT ALL RIGHT... THOUGHT HE'D AT LEAST WAIT FOR US BEFORE HE GOT STARTED.
IN LOCAL TIME, WE'VE ONLY BEEN GONE A COUPLE OF HOURS...

POLICE BOX
WE'LL JUST SLIP ABOARD BEFORE THE CO-ORDINATES WANDER TOO MUCH.
VWOORRRP
VWOORRRP

TERRIBLE TIMING, DOCTOR!
VWOORRRP
VWOORRRP
HE'S LANDING BACK IN THE GARDENS OF OSIRIS. GO, WARN HIM. WHILE ANUBEKH'S DISTRACTED.
I'LL FLY US BOTH OUT OF HERE!

NO. YOU GO. YOU'RE FASTER ON YOUR OWN.
AND WE CAN'T AFFORD FOR ANUBEKH TO FIND YOU. I'LL LISTEN SOME MORE, THEN FOLLOW.
ESTABLISHING COMMUNION.
SUTEKH, DO YOU HEAR ME? IT IS I, YOUR EARLIEST SPLINTER-SELF.
SPEAK! THE PLAN PROGRESSES?
INDEED. SEE AS I SEE...
THE SHINING HORIZON WILL SOON BE ALIGNED TO THE CIRCLE OF TRANSCENDENCE.
HURRY. I MUST BE FREED FROM THIS LIMBO.
MY PATIENCE HAS ALREADY BEEN STRETCHED BEYOND ENDURANCE.

YOU ARE GOING TO USE THE AUGMENTOR? YOU'LL FIND IT IS NOT FINISHED, FATHER.
IT AWAITS FURTHER COMPONENTS UNAVAILABLE TO ME AND IS THEREFORE USELESS.
ANUBIS... MY SON. WE ARE REUNITED AT LAST.
YOU ARE ONE OF OUR PEOPLE'S GREATEST EVER STELLAR ARCHITECTS.
I KNOW YOU ALWAYS HAVE A THOROUGH BACK-UP PLAN.
TELL ME WHAT IT IS.

YOU WANTED TO USE A TIME ENGINE... INSTEAD YOU DECIDED TO RAID ANCIENT OSIRAN STRONGHOLDS...?
HOW... ORIGINAL. AND HOW EXPRESSLY AGAINST HORUS' RULES! THERE'S HOPE FOR YOU YET.

THE TIME ENGINE!
I RECOGNIZE THE BOX!

THE PILOT OF THIS MACHINE IS KNOWN TO ME.
IF NOT FOR A STEP SIDEWAYS AT THE LAST MOMENT, I MIGHT HAVE PERISHED AT HIS HANDS.

AIII!

ALL READY?
READY.
WHERE IS EVERYONE?
AND WHAT'S WITH THE LIGHTING LEVELS? IS THE SHINING HORIZON IN POWER-SAVE MODE...?
POLICE PUBLIC CALL BOX

MAYBE IT'S SIESTA TIME.
THAT'S ODD. THE DIMENSIONAL CONDUITS ARE OPEN...
DOCTOOOOR!
DOCTOR...!
POLICE PUBLIC CALL BOX

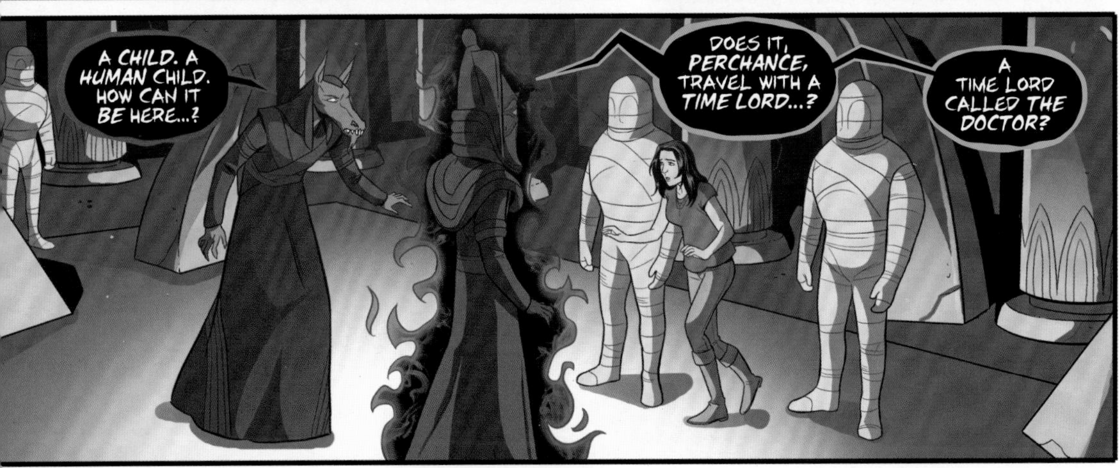
A CHILD. A HUMAN CHILD. HOW CAN IT BE HERE...?
DOES IT, PERCHANCE, TRAVEL WITH A TIME LORD...?
A TIME LORD CALLED THE DOCTOR?

THE DOCTOR, THAT INFERNAL MEDDLER, THAT DEMON OF HINDRANCE...
THANKS TO HIS INTERFERENCE I'VE HAD TO ENDURE ENTRAPMENT WITHIN THIS POCKET REALM.
HE IS THE REASON I WAS TRAPPED IN THAT ENDLESS, TEMPORAL CORRIDOR!
HE IS THE REASON I HAVE HAD TO SUFFER THE INDIGNITY OF BARTERING WITH SO-CALLED ALLIES!
HE IS THE CAUSE OF SO MANY FRUSTRATIONS.

T WILL BE ATIFYING TO VISCERATE OU, CHILD...
BUT THAT WILL BE NOTHING COMPARED TO THE PLEASURE I'LL TAKE IN METING OUT A MORE PROTRACTED DEATH TO THE DOCTOR...

NOOOO!
VORSSH
THRKKK
INTERESTING. A FLUTTERING OF RESISTANCE.
THIS INSECT HAS ENCOUNTERED AN OSIRAN BEFORE. HOW...?
WILL NOT... MUST NOT...

EXTRAORDINARY.
GABRIELLA... RUN.
CANNOT MAINTAIN CONTROL.

I SEE IT IN OUR MIND, ANUBIS... YOU CANNOT HIDE FROM ME.
YOU ACTUALLY THINK OF THIS IRRITANT... THIS PRANCING FLEA... AS... A FRIEND.
GAAAAH
VORSSH

SHE ACTUALLY ADMONISHED YOU ONCE. AND YOU ALLOWED IT.
YOU ADMIRE IT, FOR HAVING SUCH TEMERITY. YOU ACTUALLY CARE WHAT IT THINKS!
RAAAAGGH
VORSSH

YOU CARE FOR THIS ELICATE, TRANSPARENT ITTLE SACK OF BONES, BLOOD AND WATER.
THAT IS NSEEMLY FOR AN OSIRAN.
YOU DISGUST ME.

BUT THEN, ALL LIFE DISGUSTS ME.

... A FRAGMENT OF SUTEKH?
THAT'S BAD, RIGHT? I HAVE A BAD FEELING ABOUT THIS.
ANUBIS POSSESSED BY SUTEKH? VERY, VERY BAD. CATASTROPHIC.
DOROTHY... WHERE'S GABBY?
I LEFT HER THERE. SHE'S WATCHING... LISTENING...
POLICE PUBLIC CALL BOX

YOU LEFT HER... IN THE CENTRAL CORE... EAVESDROPPING ON SUTEKH?
WE SAW THE TARDIS LANDING. SHE SENT ME TO WARN YOU!

RRRRMMMMM
MOVING THE SHIP... THAT'S WHAT THE POWER DRAIN IS...
HE'S USING THE DIMENSIONAL CONDUITS TO REENERGIZE THE CIRCLE. WHY? THAT'S A ONE-WAY INBOUND TICKET!
HE'S BRINGING SOMETHING THROUGH. SOMETHING...
...OR SOMEONE!
RRRRMMMM

ALIGNMENT ACHIEVED.
NEXT ITEM...
THE ALLIES. RELEASE THEM.

RELEASE THEM? BUT THE PLAN WAS TO--
I HAVE MODIFIED THE PLAN.

THE DOCTOR HAS INTERFERED BEFORE.
HE IS EXTREMELY CUNNING... HE'S UNPREDICTABLE AND CREATIVE. WE MUST BE ON OUR GUARD.
NOTHING MUST PREVENT MY RETURN!
I SEE YOUR THINKING.
THIS WAY, WE KEEP OUR ARRANGEMENT WITH THE ALLIES...

AND IT IS USEFUL AS A DISTRACTION FOR THE DOCTOR.
EXACTLY. LET THEM THROUGH. ONE AT A TIME.

KRKKKOOOOM

DOCTOR... THAT'S...
OH NO. THAT'S...
OF COURSE. THE CIRCLE OF TRANSCENDENCE ISN'T JUST AN EXIT TO A FOUR-DIMENSIONAL UNIVERSE...
REALIGNED, IT'S A MOMENTARY KEYHOLE TO ANYWHERE. EVEN THE VOID BETWEEN UNIVERSES...

THE KING NOCTURNE!
AND THAT... THAT DRAGON. I KEPT SEEING THAT DRAGON WHEN--
I TOLD YOU. I TOLD YOU!
YES...WHEN THE TARDIS WAS ATTACKED.
IT MIGHT'VE BEEN THE TIME SENTINEL WHO WENT FISHING FOR US...

BUT IT WAS THIS LOT WHO'D BEEN WAITING...
...WHO TOOK THE OPPORTUNITY TO TRY AND TEAR US OUT OF THE SPACE-TIME CONTINUUM WITH SHEER PSYCHIC FORCE.
W-WHY?

SOME OF THEM HAVE OLD SCORES TO SETTLE.
WITH YOU? THEY HATE YOU THAT MUCH?
EVIDENTLY. I BEAT THEM.
WELL, NOT JUST ME... HAD HELP. THEY HATE EVERYONE, EVERYTHING.
BUT, Y'KNOW... THEY'RE NOT VERY NICE TO BEGIN WITH.

POLICE PUBLIC CALL BOX
POLICE
MAYBE THEY'RE SO BORING THEY HAVEN'T GOT ANYTHING BETTER TO DO THAN DWELL ON THAT.
COME ON!

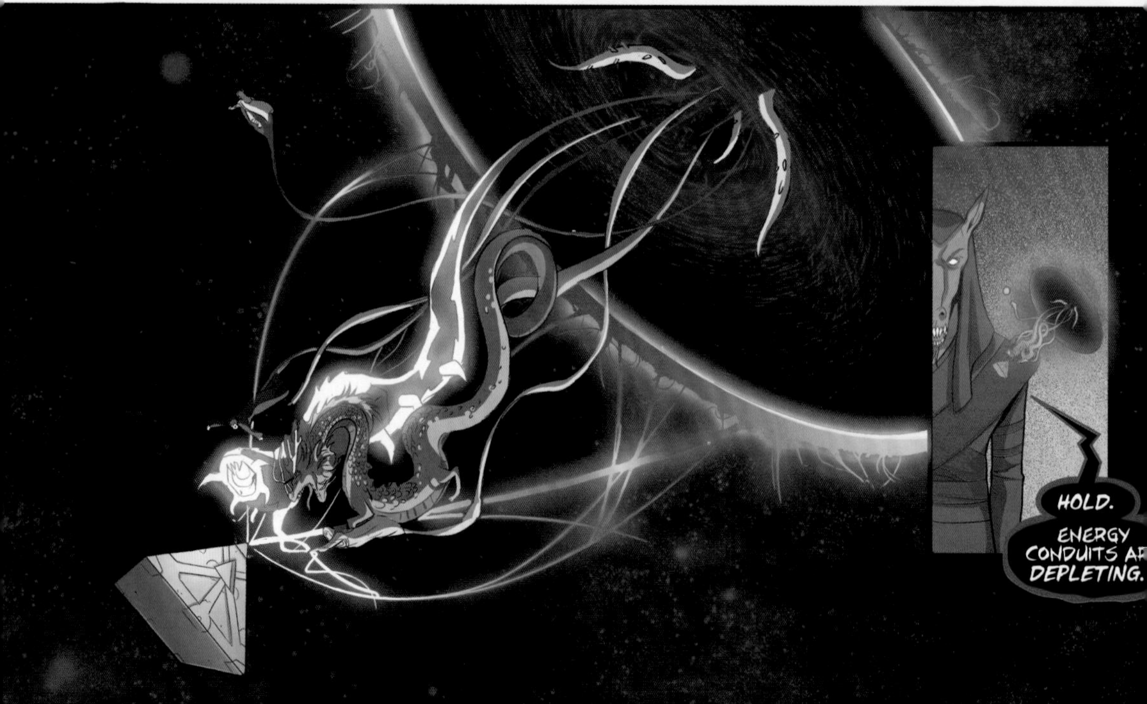
HOLD.
ENERGY CONDUITS AR
DEPLETING.

IT APPEARS THAT ONE OF OUR... "ALLIES" IS TAKING MATTERS INTO HIS OWN HANDS.
HENCE THE POWER SIPHON.
ENOUGH. LET NO OTHERS THROUGH FOR THE TIME BEING.
THEY CAN ENDURE THE EXCRUCIATING FRUSTRATION OF EXPERIENCING THE NEED FOR PATIENCE.

MAKE READY FOR MY ARRIVAL.
I WILL EXULT TO BECOME A PART OF YOU ONCE MORE. TO BECOME WHOLE!

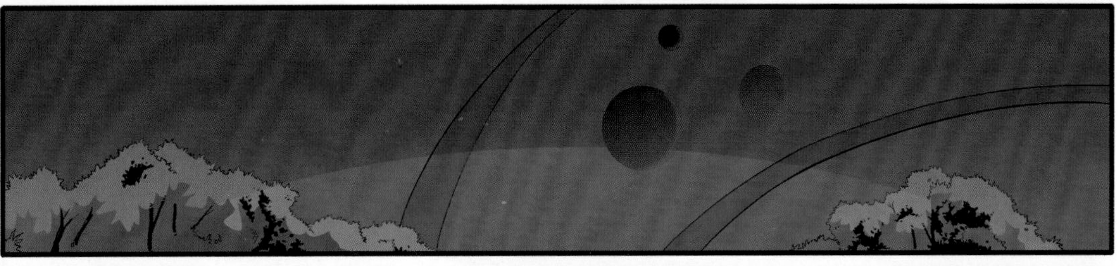

DOROTHY, PUT ME DOWN!
IF I DO, WE WON'T KEEP UP WITH HIM, HONEY!

OKAY, RIGHT, BUT I'M NOT GONNA BE MUCH USE IF I'M TOO BUSY THROWING UP...
OKAY, OKAY!

SHOULD BE SIMPLE ENOUGH TO REVERSE THE FLOW...
CAN USE THE AUGMENTOR TO...
DOCTOR...!
TIME LORD.

DOCTOR... I THINK WE JUST RAN OUT OF TIME...

MWOWBB
TIME ENOUGH TO DO THIS...
THEY'RE FROZEN!
I GET IT! YOU USED ANUBIS'S TIME DILATION AUGMENTOR TO CREATE A... A HYSTERESIS?
YUP. A DEGRADING, LOCAL TIME LOOP. BEST I CAN MANAGE...
BUT IT BUYS US A LITTLE TIME. COME ON...!
I SENSE YOU, DOCTOR. I SENSE YOUR MEDDLING...
I KNOW WHAT YOU'LL DO. YOU'LL ATTEMPT TO REVERSE THE DIMENSIONAL CONDUITS AND SEND THESE "ALLIES" OF MINE BACK FROM WHENCE THEY CAME.
YOU'LL TRY THE SAME TRICK ON ME.
THE BRIDGE IS CREATED.
YOU MAY CROSS.

I WILL NEVER FORGET YOUR FACE, DOCTOR... THE TASTE OF YOUR MENTAL ESSENCE.
I WILL NEVER FORGET YOUR BRAVADO. YOU THOUGHT IT MASKED THE STENCH OF THE FEAR YOU FELT IN MY PRESENCE...
I'VE SEEN INSIDE YOUR MIND. I'LL ALWAYS RECOGNIZE YOUR PSYCHIC IMPRINT.
YOU WERE THE LAST THING I SAW AS I LEFT THIS UNIVERSE.
IT IS ALWAYS GOOD TO HAVE AN ESCAPE HATCH, AS MY SON ANUBIS KNOWS. AS ALL OSIRANS KNOW...
AS ALL GODS AND DEVILS KNOW.
EVEN IF THAT EXIT IS A SIDEWAYS STEP TO SOME LIMBO REALM, AN ETERNALS' VOID.

SOME THERE FOR ETERNITY PASS. OTHERS DO NOT.
THE DRAGON CAME AND WENT, WHISPERING PLATITUDES AND THE POSSIBILITY OF MAKING BARGAINS...
OTHERS CAME AND WENT, EACH OF THEM CURIOUS...
EACH OF THEM CALLING THEMSELVES DEITIES OF CHAOS AND DESTRUCTION, DISGRUNTLED BY THEIR BANISHMENT TO THIS VOID...
THERE ARE A MYRIAD OF THEM HERE.
THEY SCRATCHED AND MEWLED LIKE KITTENS AT MY DOOR....
EACH OF THEM SUGGESTING A PACT, AN AGREEMENT...
BECAUSE THEY KNOW THAT I AM NATIVE TO THE UNIVERSE TO WHICH I NOW RETURN, AND THEY ARE NOT.
I AM OF NATURE, NOT FROM OUTSIDE IT. NATURE CREATED ME. SHE IS MY POWER.
I'VE WAITED SO LONG TO SHARE THE GIFTS SHE ENDOWED ME WITH.
I WANT NOTHING IN RETURN.
I WANT NOTHING, EXCEPT EVERYTHING TO BE NOTHING.
AND NOW I CROSS THE BRIDGE... HOME.
YOUR BEARING IS ASKEW... I OFFER CORRECTED CO-ORDINATES...
HOLD. I HAVE BUSINESS ELSEWHERE FIRST.
AH. OF COURSE.
I'LL RETURN SOON.
SEARCH FOR THE DOCTOR.

OTHROS MU
POPULATION: 6.8 BILLION

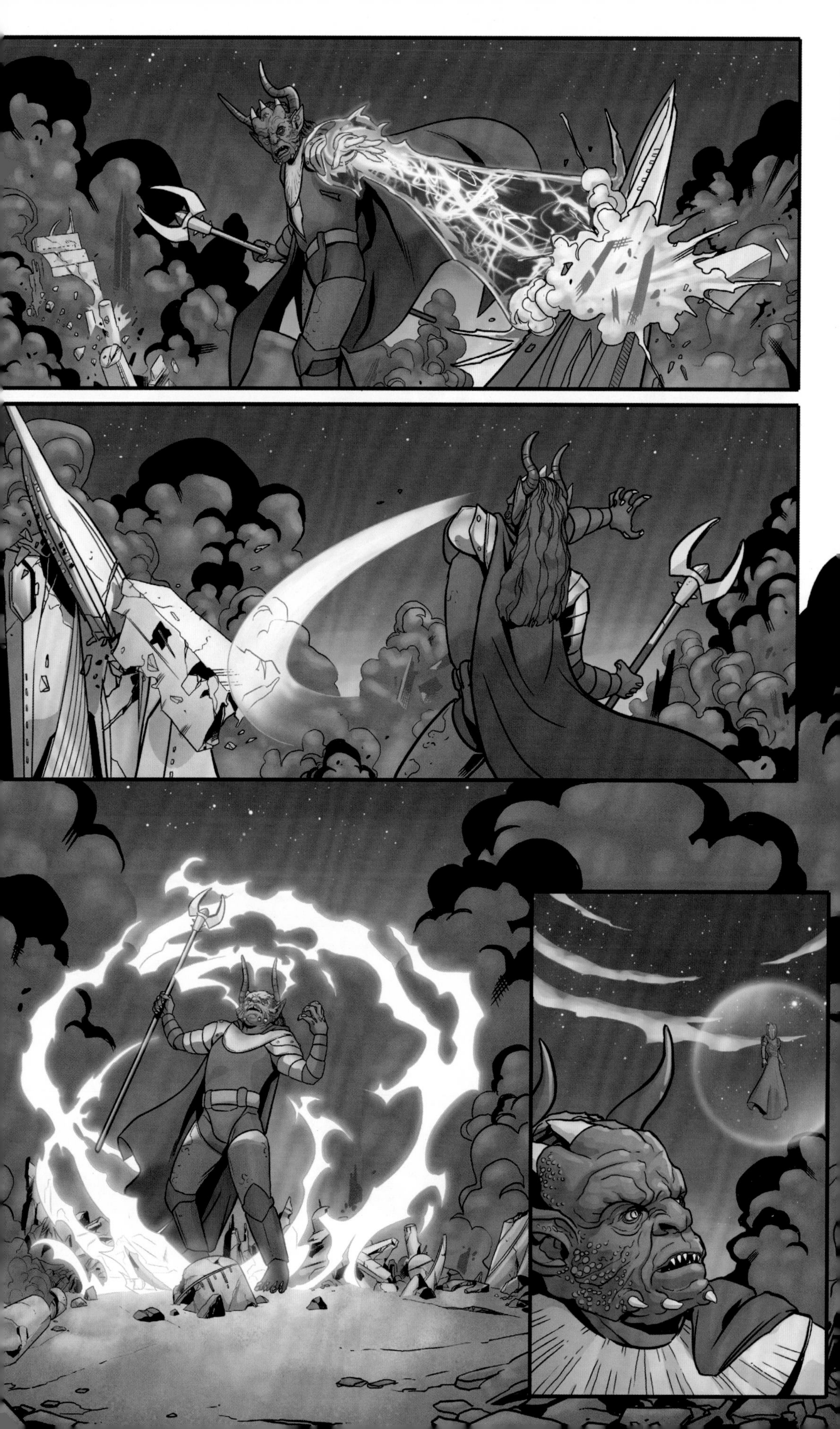

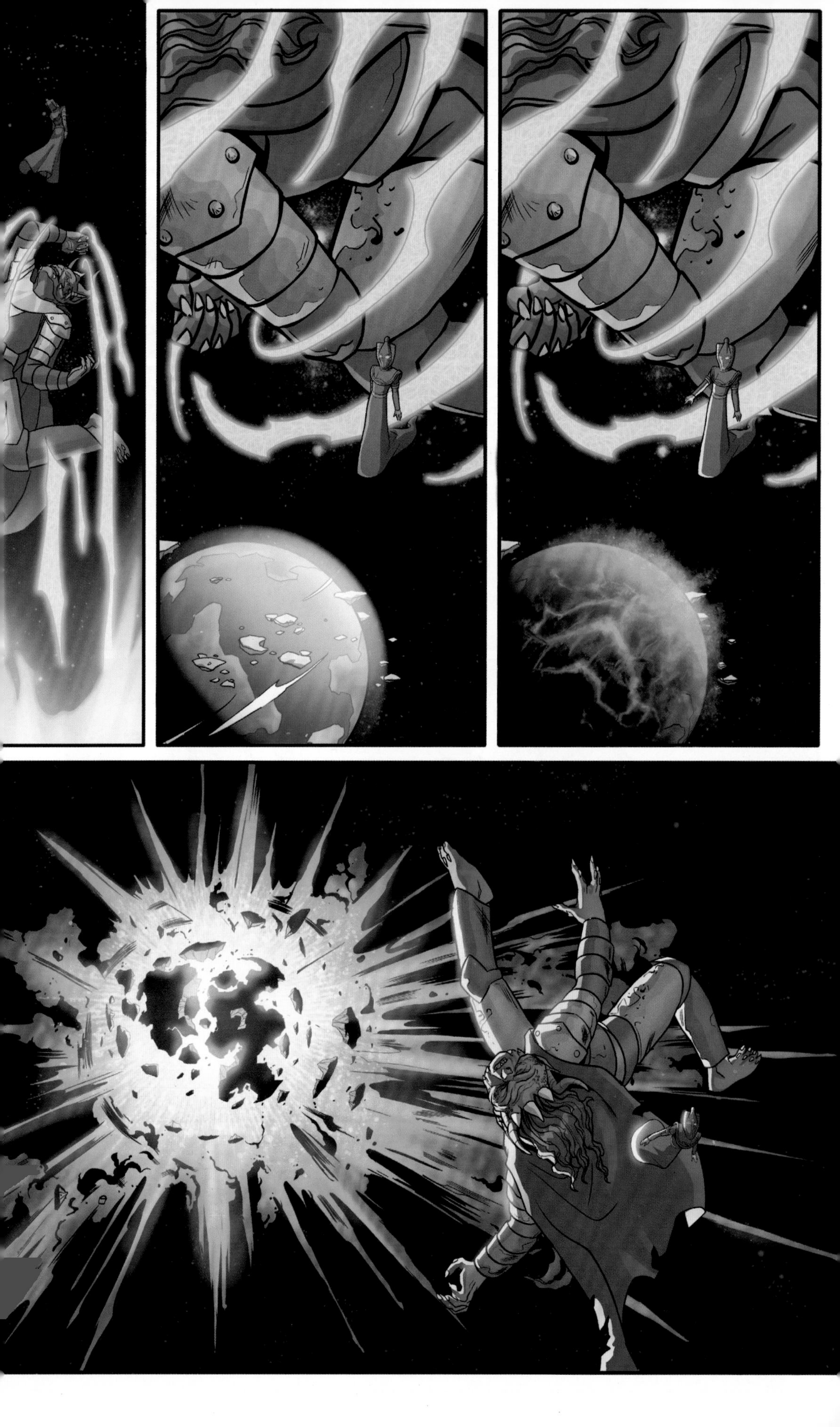

LISTEN TO ME VERY CAREFULLY.
SUTEKH IS COMING BACK HERE. I WANT YOU BOTH TO CIRCLE BACK ROUND TO THE TARDIS. STAY TOGETHER.
YOU'VE GOT THE KEY I GAVE YOU, CINDY...?
Y-YES.

NO HEROICS. DON'T TAKE THE INITIATIVE. NO LAST-MINUTE ATTEMPTS TO SAVE THE DAY... OR ME. STICK TO THE PLAN.

DOCTOR.
GREETINGS, DOCTOR. I KNOW YOU'RE HERE, ON THE SHINING HORIZON.
SHALL WE PLAY A LITTLE GAME OF CAT AND MOUSE? I DID SO LIKE THOSE CATS ON EARTH... NIMBLE LITTLE CREATURES.
THEY RESEMBLED SOME OF MY SISTERS... I DRANK DOWN SOME OF THEIR LIFE ENERGIES ONCE, AND THEY EVEN TASTED QUITE SIMILAR.

IT'S SUTEKH... THE SPLINTER OF HIS CONSCIOUSNESS, SPEAKING THROUGH ANUBIS...
MOVE.
YOU CAN BE THE CAT, IF YOU LIKE, AND I'LL BE THE MOUSE. IS THAT FAIR?
BE WARNED, THOUGH...

I'LL SNIFF YOU OUT WHEREVER YOU RUN.
THERE ARE ASPECTS OF ME EVERYWHERE.
SERVICE ROBOTS. RUN!

I AM LEGION.

IF YOU EVER GET BACK TO THAT STINKING LIMBO YOU USUALLY INHABIT, TELL YOUR LITTLE FRIENDS THAT SUTEKH WILL COME FOR THEM ALL.
I HAVE MANY NAMES, MANY GUISES. YOU MAY NOT RECOGNIZE MY COUNTENANCE WHEN NEXT WE MEET.
VENERATE AND FEAR ME.

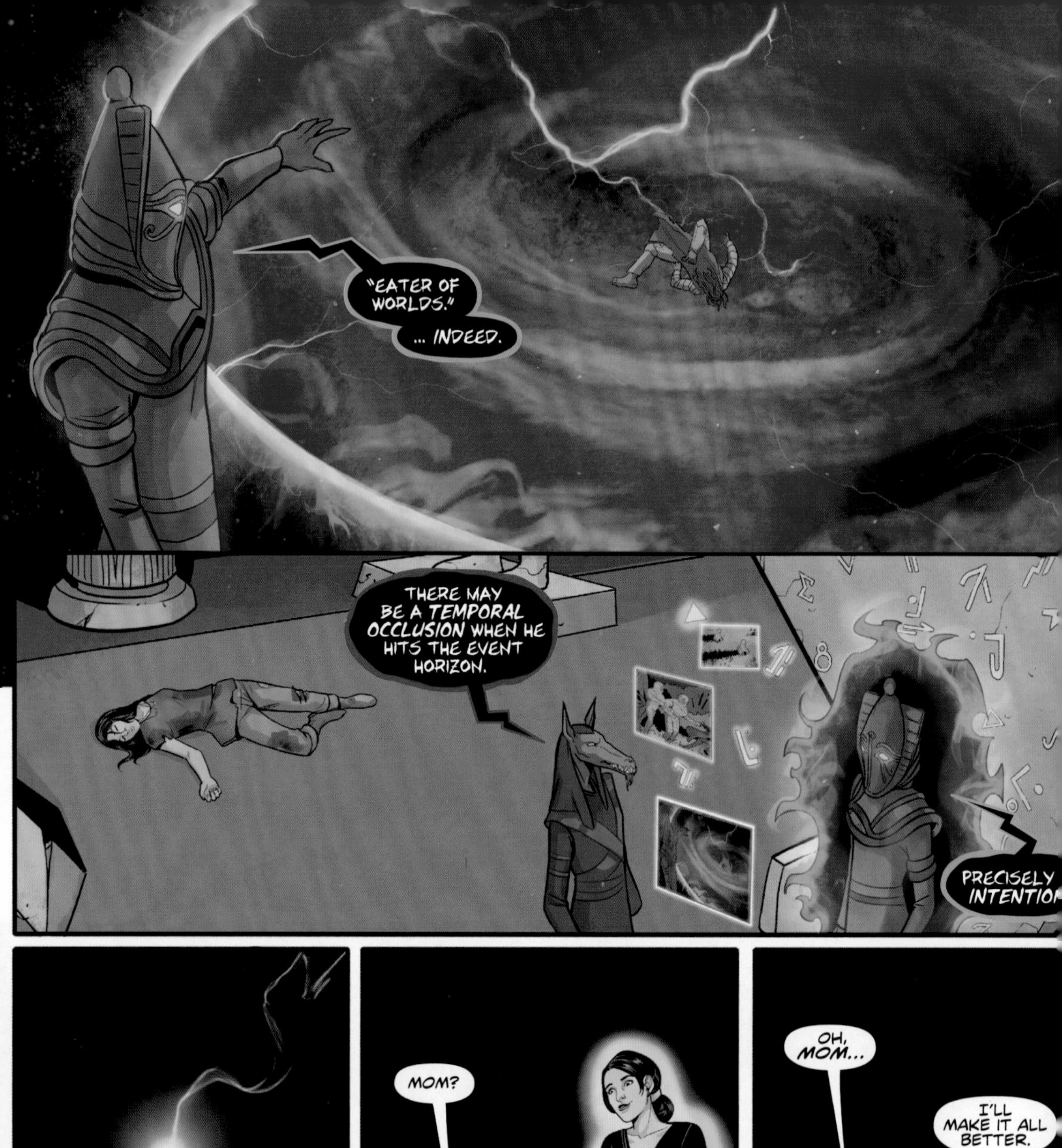
"EATER OF WORLDS."
... INDEED.
THERE MAY BE A *TEMPORAL OCCLUSION* WHEN HE HITS THE EVENT HORIZON.
PRECISELY

MOM?

OH, MOM...
I'LL MAKE IT ALL BETTER.
SSHHH

ROTHY?
GABBY, SSHHH, IT'S ALL RIGHT.
YOU'LL BE ALL RIGHT, TRUST ME...
HEAR WHAT I SAY.
YOU MUST HELP ANUBIS... HELP HIM AT THE MOMENT HE BREAKS FREE.
HELP ALL YOUR FRIENDS. HELP DOROTHY...
HELP THE DOCTOR. HE WILL KNOW WHAT TO DO.

SEE THE PROBLEM FROM ALL SIDES TO GET THE MEASURE OF IT...

...UHHHH

WHOA

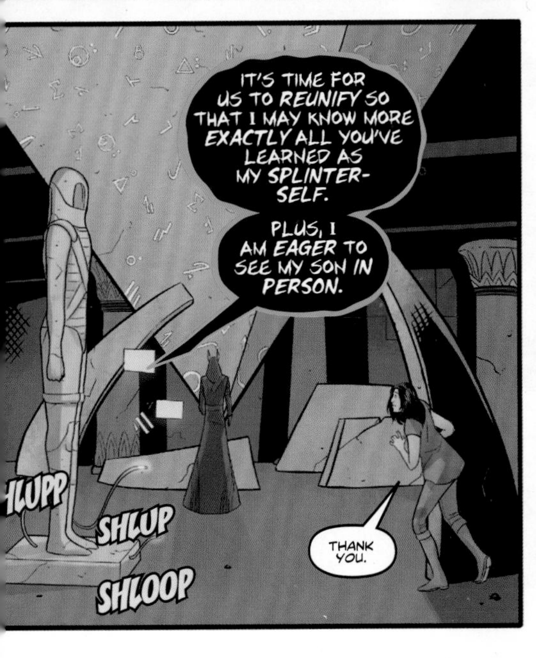

IT'S TIME FOR US TO REUNIFY SO THAT I MAY KNOW MORE EXACTLY ALL YOU'VE LEARNED AS MY SPLINTER-SELF.
PLUS, I AM EAGER TO SEE MY SON IN PERSON.
HLUPP
SHLUP
SHLOOP
THANK YOU.

I-- WE-- WILL MEET YOU IN THE GARDENS OF OSIRIS...

HUNH... HUNH

GREETINGS, CINDY. REMEMBER ME?
STILL GOT YOUR PSYCHIC EAR PLUGS?
NO? THOUGHT NOT.

I
UGHT
LIKED
TUNE.
GAR"...
T THAT
AT IT'S
LED?
ROSCOE WOULD SERENADE YOU WITH IT.
I KNOW THAT BECAUSE I CONSUMED HIM. HE'S A PART OF ME, NOW.
DOCTOR...!

...DOCTOR...!
CINDY!
GO! I'LL FINISH RIGGING THIS.
TRUST ME. I'VE LEARNED A LOT. I CAN DO IT.

OCTOR...!
IT'S TOO LATE. HE'S NOT GOING TO GET HERE IN TIME TO SAVE YOU.

THERE'S JUST NOWHERE TO RUN AND HIDE THIS TIME, FLESHLING.

WHAT HAVE WE HERE?
MUSIC TO MY EARS...?

IF I INVITE YOU INTO MY HOME, YOU REALLY SHOULD ASK BEFORE YOU TAKE ANYTHING.
THAT'S JUST SIMPLE PROTOCOL. RULES OF CONDUCT.
MANNERS.
I AM A GOD. I DO NOT ASK PERMISSION. MY SONG IS ETERNAL.
THE ONLY SONG THAT IS ETERNAL IS SILENCE.
WHAT PAINS ME MOST ABOUT MUSIC IS...
IT SOUNDS SO... ALIVE.
IT MIMICS THE INCESSANT WRITHING OF THE FOUNDATIONS OF MATTER...
ALL THOSE PATTERNS AND REPEATED MOTIFS AND VARIATIONS...
THAT ENDLESS, POINTLESS SPIRAL OF POSSIBILITY.
GRAKKKK

I WANT THE SHIFTING, MICROCOSMIC SQUIRM OF THE QUANTUM STUFF THAT YOU ARE MADE OF TO STOP.
TO BE INERT.
I WANT POSSIBILITY ITSELF TO BE IMPOTENT POWDER.
NO MORE SONGS.
BE STILL, NOW.
AS ASH. AS DUST.
THERE.
ISN'T THAT SO MUCH BETTER?
IT'S QUIET, NOW. IT'S STILL.
YOU ARE ANOTHER OF THE DOCTOR'S WAIFS...
WHY DOES HE LIKE HUMANS SO MUCH? WHAT IS HIS ATTACHMENT TO EARTH?
SPEAK. ARE YOU MUTE?
GAAAARRRGH
PLAAMM

NO!
IMPOSSIBLE!
THE PARALYSIS... NOT AGAIN...
SHRKKKK

SHRKKKK

SHRKKKK

NO.

ACKK!
VORSSSH

FRZZKKK

THIS WILL NOT HAPPEN AGAIN.
SUTEKH WILL NOT BE PARALYZED. SUTEKH WILL NOT BE IMPRISONED.

YOU CAN'T GO OUT THERE. THEY'LL KILL YOU ON SIGHT.
I'LL--

NO NEED.
GOT ANOTHER PLAN.
VREEE

THERE'S THE DOCTOR'S SIGNAL.
TIME TO SPRING THE TRAP... AND REVERSE THE DIMENSIONAL CONDUITS.

SHROOOOO

OBOY. TIME TO GO.
'BYE, DORKS. DON'T GIVE UP THE DANCING LESSONS.

SHROOOOO
PREDICTABLY ON CUE, DOCTOR.
YOU RUN THROUGH ALL THE OPTIONS. I EXPECT YOU WILL THROW THE HAND OF SUTEKH ITSELF AT ME, TOO.

I SHOULD NOT TURN MY BACK UPON YOU AGAIN, CHILD.
SPEAK.
I THOUGHT YOU WANTED QUIET.
WHAT D'YOU WANT ME TO SAY? YOU'LL KILL ME, ANYWAY.
YOU'RE THE GOD OF DEATH.

IS THAT HOW YOU PERCEIVE ME? I AM SUTEKH THE DESTROYER, YES...
BUT IF THAT IS SO, YOUR DOCTOR IS THE HIGH PRIEST OF THE DAMNED, WHO STANDS AT THE ENTRANCEWAY OF MY REALM, USHERING FOOLS TO THEIR DOOM.
YOU'RE WRONG. HE HELPS PEOPLE. HE SAVES WORLDS.
HE'S GOOD.

DOCTOR...!
WE HAVE TO MOVE. SERVITORS ARE COMING.
SOMETHING'S WRONG. SUTEKH SHOULD'VE BEEN SUCKED BACK INTO SPACE BY NOW -- BACK TOWARDS THE CIRCLE!
OH, CINDY... WHAT HAVE I DONE?

THERE'S A BLOCKAGE. SOMETHING PREVENTING THE FLOW OF ENERGY.
YOU CAN'T PLUG THE CIRCLE OF TRANSCENDENCE. IT'S NOT A BATHTUB. UNLESS...

NO...! THE EATER OF WORLDS...!

AAUUUHHH
THE DOCTOR IS GOOD?

I'VE SEEN INSIDE HIS MIND. HE'S STAINED WITH BLOOD. HE CAUSES SUFFERING.
I KNOW HE'S ON THIS SHIP. WHERE IS HE?
I END SUFFERING, BUT I WILL EXTEND YOURS INDEFINITELY IF YOU DO NOT TELL ME.
AAUUUHHH
ANUBIS....! HELP ME!

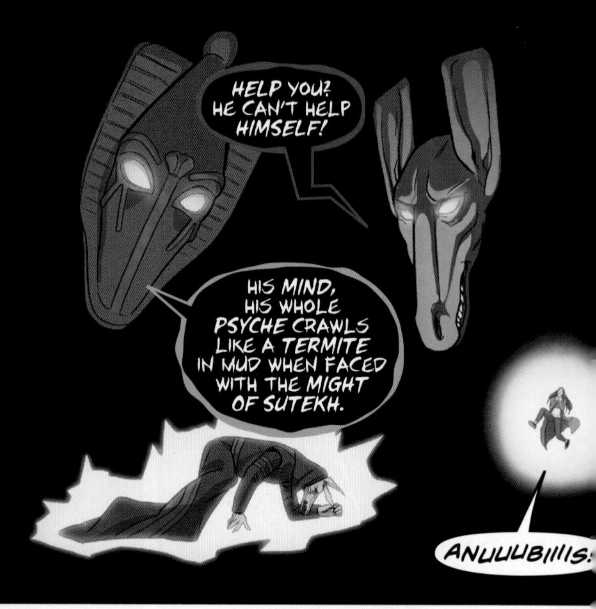
HELP YOU? HE CAN'T HELP HIMSELF!
HIS MIND, HIS WHOLE PSYCHE CRAWLS LIKE A TERMITE IN MUD WHEN FACED WITH THE MIGHT OF SUTEKH.
ANUUUBIIIIS!

GABBY, NO.
LET ME GO, DOCTOR. I HAVE TO HELP CINDY.
I SAW WHAT SUTEKH DID TO THE KING NOCTURNE. DID YOU?

AFTER NEW ORLEANS AND WUPATKI, I'M NOT GOING TO GRIEVE FOR NOCTURNES...

BUT I WOULDN'T BE ABLE TO LIVE WITH MYSELF IF I LEFT CINDY TO FACE THAT ALONE.
...SOMETIMES THERE ARE NO GOOD CHOICES, RIGHT, DOCTOR?

I'M COMING TOO.
WAIT, WAIT, LOOK -- WE CAN'T HELP CINDY IF SUTEKH KILLS US ALL.
AND DOROTHY -- WE CAN'T RISK HIM GETTING HIS HANDS ON YOU! YOU'RE THE HAND OF SUTEKH...

JUST GIVE ME A MOMENT.
WHAT DO WE DO WHEN THERE ARE NO GOOD CHOICES?
WE IMPROVISE, WE STRATEGIZE.
WE LOOK FOR NEW VARIABLES.
IT'S NOT A GAME OF CHESS. CINDY'S ALL ALONE, DOCTOR! HOW DID YOU LET THAT HAPPEN?
OH MY GOD

DOCTOR, ARE YOU WATCHING? CAN YOU SEE THIS?
I KNEW YOU WOULD TRY TO REVERSE THE DIMENSIONAL CONDUITS.
IT WAS CHILD'S PLAY TO REDIRECT THOSE ENERGIES AND USE THEM FOR MY OWN ENDS.

SEE HOW I USE THEM TO FULLY REJUVENATE MYSELF.
SEE HOW I USE MY SON'S OWN LIFE FORCE TO REVITALIZE MY OWN PSYCHE.
SUCH NOURISHMENT!

IT'S MY FAULT, ISN'T IT?
I LET HIM OUT. IT'S BECAUSE OF ME THAT SUTEKH IS HERE.
I LET SUTEKH OUT!
NOW I AM WHOLE.
SUTEKH IS ARISEN.
SUTEKH IS REBORN!

HOW DID SUTEKH'S CONSCIOUSNESS GET HERE, SO IT COULD POSSESS ANUBIS?
IT MUST'VE COME ABOARD THE SHINING HORIZON WITH THE ONLY OTHER NEW ELEMENT THAT ARRIVED RECENTLY-- AND STAYED.
ME.

A COPY OF TEKH'S CONSCIOUSNESS, CED INSIDE A QUANTUM HARVESTER...
WHICH WAS DESIGNED TO BE OPERATED BY AN OSIRAN.
INSTEAD, IT MERGED, PERMANENTLY, WITH ME. I ACTIVATED IT.
BECAUSE I WANTED YOUTH AGAIN...

ALL THIS IS BECAUSE OF MY VANITY.
I SHOULD'VE SEEN IT IN THE FLUX OF POTENTIALITIES...
DOROTHY, WITHOUT YOU, THE SITUATION COULD'VE TURNED OUT FAR WORSE.
IF SUTEKH HAD MANIFESTED AGAIN ON EARTH...

LET'S NOT THINK ABOUT THAT NOW.
WE HAVE OTHER WORRIES...
YES, WE DO. AND OTHER CHOICES.

VREEEE
AH, CHOICES, CHOICES...

FREE.
ANGRY.
BORED. UNACCEPTABLY BORED.
STAND BY, GABBY... THE VARIABLES ARE CHANGING EVERY MOMENT...
DOROTHY, CAN YOU PATCH ME INTO THE SHIP'S COMMS?
SURE, BETT THAN THAT. HAVE A SEE LINK RIGH HERE.
HELLO, SOOTY. CAN YOU HEAR ME? THIS IS SWEEP.

AS IN CLEAN SWEEP. A NICE FRESH BROOM TO BRUSH THE OLD COBWEBS AWAY.
DOCTOR! YOUR VOICE HAS CHANGED, BUT THAT SMUG TONE HAS NOT.
SOON, YOU WILL BE BLEATING FOR MERCY, I PROMISE YOU.

HELLO TOO, OTHER GODS! WELCOME TO THE SHINING HORIZON!
YOU'VE ALL BEEN BETRAYED BY SUTEKH. HE LURED YOU HERE SO I COULD PUT YOU IN A TIME LOOP.

TRICKERY. THE DOCTOR LIES!
DO I? JUST ASK THE EATER OF WORLDS IF YOU DON'T BELIEVE ME.
OH, SORRY, YOU CAN'T-- HE'S BEING USED AS A DOOR STOP RIGHT NOW.

SOOTY HERE WEDGED HIS HEAD RIGHT UP THE CIRCLE OF TRANSCENDENCE.
LOOK, SEE?
DOCTOR, WHEN I FIND YOU, I WILL TURN YOU INSIDE OUT.
WHEN I MAKE YOU EXPEL YOUR HEARTS THROUGH YOUR OWN MOUTH, YOU'LL BE LESS TALKATIVE.

THAT'S IT, SOOTY, YOU COME AND FIND ME...
SHROWWWW
OOOOOOF

...MAYBE WHEN YOU'RE LESS BUSY.

HEY, OTHER GODS... DON'T FORGET, SUTEKH IS AN ENEMY OF ALL LIFE.
AND, IN THIS REALITY, YOU COUNT AS LIFE, SO... WORK IT OUT FOR YOURSELVES.
SHROWWWW

INCOMPETENTS. RANK AMATEURS.
YOU THINK TO COMPARE YOURSELVES TO ME?
ARGGGKKK
WE WILL SEE, SUTEKH, WE WILL S--
EEEEEEE

S ANUBIS
VEN STILL
ALIVE?
JUST ABOUT. WE HAVE TO GET HIM TO A SEEKER NODE.
W-WHAT'S A SEEKER NODE?
TRUST ME, IT'LL DO THE JOB.

MAYBE I CAN LIFT HIM THIS WAY...
OH, GOSH. LOOK AT YOU.

I HAVE TO HELP--
NOPE. WE HAVE TO LEAD THESE SERVITORS AWAY FROM THEM.
RUN!

LOOK AFTER MY POOR DOGFACE, GABBY.
DON'T WORRY, THEY KNOW WHAT TO DO.

SONIC... WARNING LIGHT.
CHANGE COURSE...! ON'T WANT TO UN INTO MORE SERVITORS.
D'YOU THINK WE'LL GET OUT OF THIS ALIVE?
WE MIGHT DIE HERE.

LOOK AT THEM, HER AND CINDY. SUCH INCREDIBLE LOYALTY TO EACH OTHER.
WISH I'D HAD SOMETHING LIKE THAT...
YOU HAD VIVIAN.

I EMPLOYED VIVIAN. SHE WAS DEVOTED TO ME, YES, BUT I LEFT HER SOON AS... AS SOON AS MY YOUTH WAS RESTORED.
BESIDES, THAT'S NOT WHAT I MEAN... AND YOU KNOW IT.

THEY'RE KIDS, DOCTOR. I LOOK LIKE ONE, BUT I'M NOT.
AND NEITHER ARE YOU.

IF WE-- IF THEY COME THROUGH THIS ALIVE, YOU NEED TO GIVE THEM SOME ROOM.
STOP MAKING THEM CHASE THROUGH THE UNIVERSE AFTER YOU ALL THE TIME AND LET THEM UNDERSTAND WHERE THEY ARE, Y'KNOW?

BECAUSE YOU KNOW HOW THEY BOTH FEEL ABOUT YOU. THEY'D FOLLOW YOU OVER A CLIFF.
DON'T ABUSE THAT TRUST.

SERIOUSLY, HOW MANY TIMES CAN WE KEEP ESCAPING?
CIN, NOW'S REALLY NOT THE TIME--

NO, IT'S TOTALLY THE TIME. MIGHT NOT GET ANOTHER CHANCE.
THANKS FOR COMING BACK FOR ME.
YOU'D HAVE DONE THE SAME FOR ME. WE'RE BEST FRIENDS.

GHT, YEAH. SSED YOU SO D WHEN YOU FT... BOTH TIMES.
AT FIRST I THOUGHT MAYBE I WAS JUST JEALOUS, OR JUST HURT BY THE IDEA THAT MAYBE YOU DIDN'T WANT TO COME BACK...
I JUST COULDN'T BEAR THE THOUGHT OF YOU NOT BEING AROUND.
THAT'S WHY I FOLLOWED YOU ONTO THE TARDIS.

NOT 'CAUSE THE CTOR PROMISES THE UNIVERSE...?
IS THAT WHY YOU STOPPED LLING ME "BABY" EVERY FIVE MINUTES?
CIN, I LOVE YOU OO. I REALLY JUST TELL ME OW ROSCOE FITS IN.
YOU'RE NOT TAKING THIS SERIOUSLY AT ALL.

I AM, I REALLY AM. ASIDE FROM JUST TRYING TO SURVIVE HERE...
I'M JUST NOT SURE WHETHER YOU'RE TELLING ME THAT YOU LOVE ME ...OR THAT YOU'RE IN LOVE WITH ME.
I... I'M NOT BRAVE LIKE YOU. I NEED YOUR BRAVERY.

ROSCOE... YEAH, IT WAS LIKE SOME CORNY OL' SONG -- LIKE MY HEART OPENED UP AND HE JUST WALKED RIGHT IN.
IT WAS LIKE HE KNEW ME, LET ME SEE THINGS IN NEW WAYS. I REALLY FELL.
HE WAS JUST SO GOOD AND TRUE, SO SWEET AND KIND-- HE REALLY DID JUST WANT TO MAKE MUSIC.

LIKE YOU... WHEN YOU JUST WANTED TO MAKE ART. TO BE CREATIVE.
NOW LOOK AT YOU. YOU'RE A... A STAR WARRIOR, ALL COMPETENT AND SCARY, WITH ENERGY BUTTERFLIES COMING OUT OF YOU.
YOU'VE EVOLVED.

HAVE I? I NEARLY DIED EARLIER TODAY.
ANUBIS SAVED ME, THE SEEKER REVIVED ME. HEALED ME. BUT THAT GETS YOU THINKING...
I MAY HAVE EVOLVED... BUT I DON'T WANT TO BE A WEAPON.
I STILL WANT TO BE AN ARTIST.

I DO LOVE YOU, CINDY.
BUT WHAT I'M ALWAYS TRYING TO GET YOU TO SEE... WHAT ROSCOE SAW... IS THAT YOU DON'T NEED ME TO GET BY.
YEAH, BUT THE DOCTOR--

THE DOCTOR TRUSTS YOU IMPLICITLY. HE'S ALWAYS SAYING SO. HE KNOWS YOU'RE BRAVE.
ME TOO. YOU JUST DON'T HEAR IT.
NOW, CAN WE TALK ABOUT THIS LATER AND GET ANUBIS SOMEWHERE WE CAN HELP HIM?

HOW SWEET.
TWO LITTLE HUMANS NURSING AN OSIRAN INVALID...

THIS IS MY
OMECOMING, MY
CONNECTION WITH
E MOST PRIMAL,
TERIAL FORCES
N EXISTENCE.
I AM MORE POWERFUL THAN ANY SO-CALLED DEITY FROM OUTSIDE NATURE.
SUTEKH...
I NEVER RENEGED ON OUR ORIGINAL ARRANGEMENT.

I WILL CONTINUE TO ACT IN YOUR INTERESTS, IF YOU WISH IT.
ALL I ASK IS THAT YOU ALLOW ME SAFE PASSAGE FROM THIS PLACE.
AS A SHOW OF GOOD FAITH, I BRING YOU A GIFT.
WHAT DO YOU HAVE THAT I COULD POSSIBLY WANT, DRAGON?

THESE.

YOU NEED TO UNBLOCK THE CIRCLE.
YES. WITH SOMETHING THAT'S IMMUNE TO THE FORCES AT THE CIRCLE'S EVENT HORIZON...
THERE'S STILL A CHANCE I CAN RIG ANUBIS' TIME AUGMENTOR TO FLUSH SUTEKH BACK THE WAY HE CAME...

YOU CAN'T USE THIS SHIP-- THE STRESSES WILL TEAR IT APART -- AND THE TIME AUGMENTOR ISN'T FINISHED YET.
YOU CAN ONLY USE IT AS AN ACCELERATOR.
THAT LEAVES A TIME ENGINE... YOUR TARDIS.
DOROTHY, THERE ARE ALWAYS OPTIONS.

I KNOW. THERE'S A WHOLE SIDEWAYS MULTIVERSE OF 'EM OUT THERE.
I JUST DON'T LIKE WHERE YOUR IMPROVISATION IS HEADING.
DOROTHY, WE'RE WASTI TIME. WE--

HEAR ME, DOCTOR.
NO MORE CAT-AND-MOUSE. NO MORE DISTRACTIONS. NO MORE SONGS OF FREEDOM.

I HAVE YOUR HUMAN PETS-- YOUR KITH, YOUR KI THEY WILL BE THE FIRST OF THEIR KIND TO DIE...
I WILL TURN YOUR MOST FAVORED WORLD TO DUST...

AND EARTH WILL JUST BE THE BEGINNING.
THIS WILL HAPPEN IMMEDIATELY UNLESS YOU FACE ME NOW, DOCTOR.

ALL RIGHT... I'M ON MY WAY.
YOU *WIN*, SUTEKH.
WHY EVEN *RETURN*, SUTEKH? FOR *REVENGE?* VHY SO CRUEL WITH IT?
POLICE BOX
HOW DO YOU MAKE THE DARKNESS *BEARABLE?*
THERE *ARE* ALTERNATIVES...

EVIL AND CRUELTY ARE *INEVITABLE*, DOCTOR.
THEY ARE AS EMERGENT *FROM* LIFE AS *LIFE ITSELF* IS FROM THE VERY *QUANTUM STUFF* OF THE UNIVERSE.
I SIMPLY TAKE THEM TO THEIR *LOGICAL ENDS.*
THOSE ENDS ARE *DESPAIR*, THE DEBRIS OF *POSSIBILITY*, AND INEVITABLY...
DUST... *DARKNESS.*

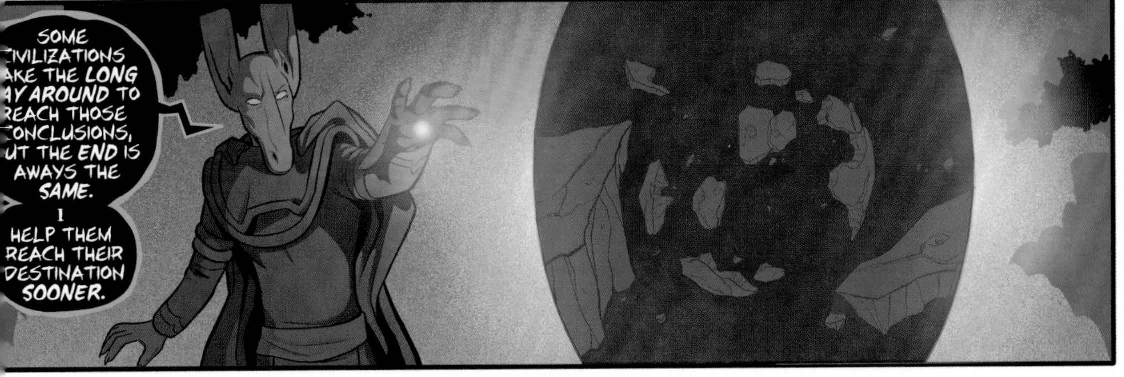

SOME IVILIZATIONS AKE THE *LONG* AY *AROUND* TO REACH THOSE ONCLUSIONS, UT THE *END* IS AWAYS THE *SAME.*
I HELP THEM REACH THEIR DESTINATION *SOONER.*

I LIBERATE THEM FROM THE SQUALOR AND ANXIETY OF THEIR EXISTENCE AND GIVE THEM THE CERTAINTY OF DEATH.
THE EMBRACE OF SUTEKH IS A GIFT.

I END SUFFERING, DOCTOR.
I AM GOOD.
I GAVE NO PERMISSION FOR YOU TO LEAVE, DRAGON.
I KEPT MY PROMISE OSIRAN. OU BUSINESS DONE.

NNNNNNNNNNNN
INDEED. FOR THAT, I THANK YOU.
HERE IS YOUR REWARD.

ALL THAT COLD LOGIC OF YOURS, SUTEKH... IT ISN'T SO INSCRUTABLE.
BUT YOU'RE WRONG. THE END ISN'T ALWAYS THE SAME. THERE ARE ALWAYS CHOICES. THERE IS ALWAYS HOPE.
SOME BEINGS TRANSCEND WAR, GREED, FEAR...

TO WHAT END, CTOR? THEY TRANSCEND UNIVERSE TO BECOME... INFORMATION?
TO BECOME A RECORDING? TO BECOME ENLIGHTENED?
TO HAVE INFINITE LIVES WITHOUT WILL OR MEANING?

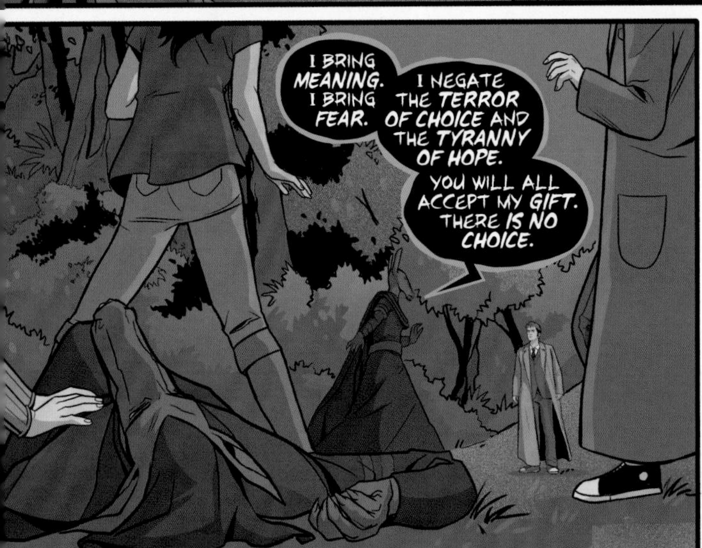
I BRING MEANING. I BRING FEAR.
I NEGATE THE TERROR OF CHOICE AND THE TYRANNY OF HOPE.
YOU WILL ALL ACCEPT MY GIFT. THERE IS NO CHOICE.

BUT ENOUGH TALK.
WHERE IS THE HAND OF SUTEKH? I KNOW IT'S HERE.

GUHHH
SHRATTT
SHROOOT

ASTOUNDING. YOU CHOOSE YOUR FRIENDS WELL, DOCTOR...
INSECTS WHO WON'T STAY SQUASHED.

RRRRMMMM
BUT YOU SEE, NONE OF THIS WILL WORK, BECAUSE IT'S SO EASY TO PREDICT YOUR PLANS.
I KNOW THAT YOU WENT BACK TO PHAESTER OSIRIS TO COLLECT PARTS FOR MY SON'S TIME AUGMENTOR.
OF COURSE YOU WOULD BRING BACK SOME INSURANCE. THAT'S HOW YOU THINK.

EVEN NOW YOU ARE CALCULATING ANOTHER DISTRACTION...
SO THEN YOU CAN RUN FOR YOUR BOX AND ATTEMPT TO CATAPAULT ME BACK THROUGH THE CIRCLE OF TRANSCENDENCE...

WHAT WILL YOU THROW AT ME NEXT? MY OWN HAND OF SUTEKH? I KNOW IT'S HERE.
WHERE HAVE YOU HIDDEN IT?

WHA--?
SURPRISE!
NOT HIDING. RIGHT HERE IN PLAIN SIGHT, HONEY.
YOU CAN REDUCE A WORLD TO RUBBLE, BUT YOU CAN'T TELL WHEN SOMEONE'S IN THE SAME ROOM AS YOU.

YOU SHOULD BE ROUD -- ANUBIS WAS STRONG ENOUGH TO KEEP WHAT I'VE BECOME A SECRET FROM YOU.
HE'S PROTECTED THE WHOLE UNIVERSE FROM YOU AND YOUR LEGACY FOR EONS.
I'M THE ANCESTRAL HEIRLOOM, DESIGNED TO MERGE WITH ANY OF YOU.
EXCEPT NOW I'M A HUMAN-OSIRAN HYBRID AND IF I TRY THAT...
IT'LL HURT US BOTH.
STILL, WE'RE FAMILY, AREN'T WE?
AARRHHNNNNNN
THIS IS WHAT YOU WANTED, SUTEKH.
SHALL WE GET ACQUAINTED, ONEY? MY, WHAT BIG EARS YOU HAVE.
DOROTHY, NO!
DOROTHY...?

GABBY, HONEY, THE CTOR WAS GOING TO SACRIFICE HIMSELF AND THE TARDIS.
HE'D SAVE THE UNIVERSE... HE'D SAVE EVERYONE BUT HIMSELF.
BUT I THINK Y'ALL AND THE UNIVERSE NEED HIM.
RAAAARGH

THAT LEFT ONLY ONE OPTION.
A QUANTUM HARVESTER CAN NAVIGATE THE CIRCLE OF TRANSCENDENCE WITHOUT BREAKING ANYTHING...
RIGHT, DOCTOR?
CINDY, BY THE FOUNTAIN... LEFT YOU SOMETHING.

DOCTOR. ACTIVATE THE AUGMENTOR. NOW. IT'S THE ONLY CHANCE.
LOVE YOU GUYS. LOOK AFTER OL' DOGFACE FOR ME. HE'LL NEED YOU.
TELL HIM... I LOVED HIM TOO. MORE'N HE'LL EVER--
DOROTHY...
DOCTOOORRRRR
I'M SO SORRY
NOOOOOOOO
VREEEE

CLICK YOUR HEELS, SUTEKH, HONEY...
THERE'S NO PLACE LIKE HOME.
RRRRMMMMM

DOCTOR...?

DOROTHY!
...GABBY?
IT"S ALL RIGHT. IT'S OKAY.
SHLUPPP
SHLUPPP
WHAT DID SHE PUT INTO ME? NANO-NURSES?
I DUNNO. BUT IF THEY'RE IN YOU, THEY'RE IN ME, TOO.
WHAT?
THE SEEKER HEALED ME, EARLIER.
IS THAT BAD?
DUNNO. DON'T THINK SO. BUT IF IT IS, WE CAN FIX IT.
WHERE'S CINDY? WHERE'S ANUBIS...?

CINDY'S FINE. SHE'S DOWN BY THE FOUNTAIN. SHE SPENDS A BIT OF TIME THERE, NOW.
TIME? HOW LONG HAVE I BEEN OUT?
A FEW DAYS. YOU CAUGHT SOME DEBRIS. WE WERE HIT BY A... A SHOCKWAVE, I GUESS...?

THE SEEKER GOT EVERYTHING UP AND RUNNING AGAIN.
THE CIRCLE'S FINE, THE SHIP'S FINE. NO TRACE OF SUTEKH.
I'LL CHECK THAT FOR MYSELF!

YOUR EYES ARE RED.
YUP. DONE A LOT OF CRYING OVER THE PAST COUPLE OF DAYS.

DOCTOR... THERE'S SOMETHING YOU NEED TO *KNOW* ABOUT ANUBIS.
HE DOESN'T REMEMBER ANYTHING. WELL... NOT MUCH.
OH...?
DOCTOR!

DOCTOR, YOU'RE *ALL RIGHT!*
WE WERE *WORRIED!*

I'M *FINE.*
WHAT'S THAT *MUSIC...?*

THE SEEKER CONJURED UP A TURNTABLE.
I THOUGHT IT WAS THE KING NOCTURNE MESSING WITH MY HEAD WHEN I HEARD 'SUGAR' THROUGH ONE OF DOROTHY'S WINDOWS TO PARALLEL WORLDS...

IN ANOTHER UNIVERSE, HE LIVED. HE LIVED, AND HE BECAME A JAZZ LEGEND.
ROSCOE RUSKIN...!
HOW ABOUT THAT!
DOROTHY SOMEHOW PULLED THESE THROUGH FROM A PARALLEL REALITY...!

YOU SAVED US. YOU KNOW THAT, DON'T YOU? YOU SAVED EVERYONE AND EVERYTHING FROM SUTEKH.
BUT NOT DOROTHY.
I COULDN'T... I WOULDN'T... I MEAN, I TRIED...

I'VE THOUGHT ABOUT... I'VE WONDERED IF -- MAYBE THERE'S OTHER DOROTHY OUT THERE TOO.
BUT EVEN IF THERE IS, OUR DOROTHY BELL WAS ONE OF A KIND.
SHE CERTAINLY WAS.

WE HAVE A LOT TO TALK ABOUT.
YEAH. MAYBE... MAYBE WE SHOULD TAKE A LITTLE TIME TO DO THAT.

HELLO...!

DOCTOR... THIS IS NEWBIS.
ARE YOU FEELING BETTER, DOCTOR? I'VE BEEN SO LOOKING FORWARD TO MEETING YOU!
WOULD YOU LIKE SOME BOOJI JUICE? IT'S AN OSIRAN DELICACY, I THINK.

WE FOUND HIM LIKE THAT. DOROTHY... SHE MUST'VE FOUND A WAY TO COMPLETELY REJUVENATE HIM.
SHE REALLY WAS A 'FOUNTAIN OF YOUTH'...

NEWBIS! NOOBIS...? WELL, I'M VERY PLEASED TO MEET YOU!
LOOK AT YOU! MY, MY!

THE END... FOR NOW!

HONE
OF

ONE
F
ANCE
DIATELY
RS
CALLS
OPEN

WOORRRP
WOORRRP
DOCTOR!!!!!

WHAT'S HAPPENING?!?
NOTHING MAJOR -- JUST A BIT OF DIMENSIONAL TURBULENCE.
PHEW!

WHICH SET OFF THE RANDOMIZER!
THE WHAT?!?

CLUE'S IN THE NAME!
RANDOMLY SETS CO-ORDINATES FOR ANYWHERE IN TIME AND SPACE.
AND THEN--

--DEPOSITS YOU THERE.
PING

LIKE PRESSING SHUFFLE ON AN iPOD.
I PREFER A GOOD PLAYLIST.
PFFT! EVERYONE'S A CRITIC.

POLICE PUBLIC CALL BOX
RANDOM IS GOOD.
SURPRISES ARE GOOD.
AND RANDOM SURPRISES ARE EVEN--
UNDERGROU
OLD STRE
--BETTER.
POLICE PUBLIC CALL BOX
LONDON!!! FINALLY!
NOW THAT'S A SHUFFLE I CAN GET BEHIND!

CINDY'S ONNA *FLIP* EN SHE HEARS WHAT SHE'S MISSE--
WE NEED TO *LEAVE*.
WHAT?!

US. LEAVE. *NOW*.
BUT WE'VE ONLY JUST ARRIVED!
YEAH, AND NOW WE'RE *GOING*.
POLICE PUBLIC CALL BOX

DOCTOR?!
THIS ISN'T *LIKE* YOU!

ISN'T IT?
HOW WOULD YOU KNOW, GABBY?
WHAT DO YOU *REALLY* KNOW ABOUT ME?!

IIIEEEEEEEEEE!

...I KNOW YOU WON'T IGNORE A CRY FOR HELP.

TOLD YA!
DON'T GET ANY *IDEAS.* WE WON'T BE HANGING AROUND.
TAXI
BEEP
BEE

I *OPENED* THE *DOOR* AND THERE IT WAS!
A FLIPPIN' *MONSTER*...IN THE *STOCKROOM!*

...MAYBE WE CAN STAY FOR *FIVE MINUTES.*
YES!!!
SECURITY

JUST A FLYING VISIT.
WHATEVER YOU SAY, BOSS!

THE TRAVELERS ARE IN OUR REACH.
EXCELLENT.
SOON THE TIME LORD AND HIS PET WIL CROSS THE THRESHOLD...

...AND THE DOORS CAN FINALLY OPEN!

RIDDLE ME THIS...

"WHEN IS A
STOCKROOM, NOT A STOCKROOM?"
SERIOUSLY?
MOSTLY.
VRRRR VRRRR
THAT'S DEBATABLE.

OUCH!
WANT TO KNOW THE ANSWER?
VRRRR
IF YOU INSIST.

"WHEN IT'S A DOORWAY TO ANOTHER DIMENSION!"
SKREEEE
IS IT... ACTUALLY HERE?

THE EXILE...THEY WILL NEED OUR HELP AGAINST HIM.
AGREED.

NO.
JUST A 4-D ECHO.

SIMPLE EXCITATION OF THE RESIDUAL DIMENSIONAL BLEED MEANS WE CAN GET A LOOK AT SQUIDDY HERE--

--WHILE I LOCK ONTO WHAT ALLOWED HIM TO BREAK ON THROUGH FROM THE OTHER SIDE.
WHICH WAS?
HAVEN'T THE FOGGIEST--

--BUT AT LEAST NOW I KNOW WHERE TO LOOK.
BLIP
BLIP

THE KEY.
CUTTING EDGE THINK-TANK ESTABLISHED BY TECH ENTREPRENEUR AARON CROSSLAND.

WENT BUST SIX MONTHS AGO.
NOW THE SITE OF MYSTERIOUS ALIEN SIGNALS.
SHALL WE?
K-CHIK
THIS IS... WEIRD.
THOUGH NOT AS WEIRD AS THE WAY YOU WERE BEHAVING EARLIER.
YUP.
WHY'S BEING LONDON SUCH A PROBLEM?
BAD STUFF ALWAYS HAPPENS HERE.
BAD STUFF HAPPENS EVERYWHERE.
NOT TO ME!
TSK!
DESPITE THE DEBONAIR FRONT--

...YOU'RE REALLY QUITE AN *AGGRESSIVE* LITTLE *DOCTOR,* AREN'T YOU?

DOCTOR... HOW... HOW COME HE KNOWS YOUR NAME?!
GETTING TO THAT.
MISTER CROSSLAND PRESUME?

YES, I AM.
WELCOME TO *THE KEY.*
AS YOU CAN SEE, I'M IN THE MIDDLE OF A RENOVATION.

LONG WAY TO GO, BY THE LOOKS OF IT...!
OH, NO -- MY *PARTNER* AND I ARE... ALREADY ENTERING THE FINAL STAGES.
DOCTOR...?

WE'VE JUS BEEN WAITI FOR THE RIG *CONTRACT* TO COME AL AND FINISH O THE JOB.

HOW -- HOW'S HE... DOING THAT?
I DON'T THINK IT'S *HIM,* GABBY.

BUT NOW THAT YOU'RE HERE... WELL, THE FINAL STAGE CAN TRULY BEGIN!

THIS IS *BAD.*
REALLY?
AND THERE I WAS THINKING EVERYTHING WAS HUNKY DORY!
HE'S LIKE NE OF THOSE HINGS WE SAW ARLIER -- JUST BIGGER AND REDDER.
I'D *NOTICED!*
HE'S GIVING OFF *MASSIVE* PSIONIC POWER READINGS.

WHAT IS IT...?
NEXT ON THE LIST.
WHO ARE YOU?

WE ARE THE REACH.
...
PERSONALLY, I RECKON 'OCTONAUT' MIGHT'VE BEEN A BETTER NAME... BUT IT'S PROBABLY ALREADY TAKEN.

WHAT DO YOU WANT?
WHAT ALL EXILES WANT, DOCTOR.
TO REACH HOME AGAIN.
AND HOW DO YOU PLAN TO DO THAT?

BY BREAKING YOUR HEART!

DOCTOR, WHAT'S HE DOING?!?
CROSSLAND... REACH... WHATEVER YOU CALL YOURSELF...

PUT HER DOWN!!!

IF YOU INSIST!

NOOOOOOO!
DOCTORRRRR!!

RRGGGGGGHHH!
GABBY!!

SLAM

GABBY!!!!!

HOW DOES IT FEEL, DOCTOR?
ANOTHER COMPANION LOST... THROUGH THE REVOLVING DOOR OF A LIFE WITH YOU?
WHERE IS SHE?

TUMBLING IN THE SPA BETWEEN SPACES.
HOWEVER, WITH YOU POWER, IF Y WERE TO FOL HER... YOU MI GET LUCKY AN ABLE TO BR HER HOME

THIS IS UNDOUBTEDLY A TRAP.
LIKE EVERYTHING ELSE SINCE WE ARRIVED HERE.

THOUGH WHAT CHOICE DO I HAVE?

THWUNK
OOOOF!

OK, DOCTOR... WHERE ARE WE?
AND WHERE'S--

GABBY?!!!

IT'S ALRIGHT, GABBY.
EVERYTHING'S GOING TO BE ALRIG--

MARTHA?!

STUN MINE.

UNNNGHH...
TSK! WHAT DID I TELL YOU ABOUT DOING UNIT FIELDWORK, DR JONES?
KLIK SCHLURK KLIK

LET ME GUESS: YOU'RE THE ONE WHO HURT MY FRIEND HERE?
KLIK
SCHLURK
KLIK
EITHER WAY...

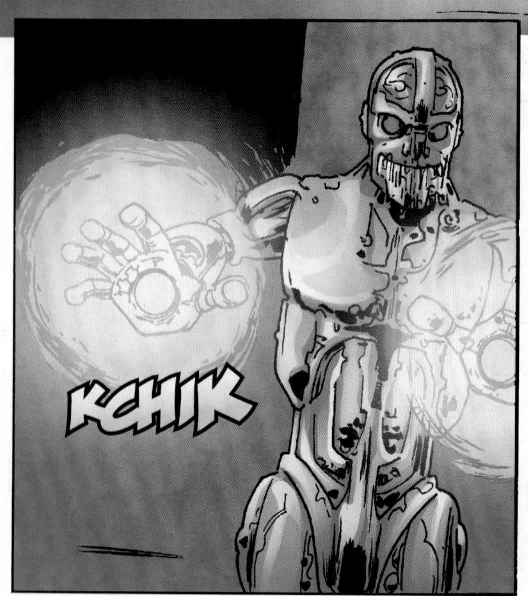
KCHIK

...BAD MOVE!
KABOOM

KLI..K....
SCHLURK...
URRRGGGH...
I'M SORRY, MARTHA, BUT I CAN'T STICK AROUND.
THERE'S SOMEONE ELSE OUT THERE THAT I NEED TO FIND.

THAT'S OUR STORY IN A NUTSHELL.
FZZZK

"I KNOW YOU'LL UNDERSTAND."
HUH?

WHAT DO YOU MEAN YOU 'THREW IT AWAY'?
WHAT?!

WHAT I SAID!
IF YOU LEAVE THINGS LYING AROUND, DON'T BE SURPRISED IF THEY END UP IN THE BIN!

WELL, ISN'T THAT WIZARD!
WHAT ABOUT MY PURSE?
NO...

IT'S IN THE FRONT ROOM!

CAN'T DEAL WITH THIS... NOT HERE... NOT NOW...
WELL, THAT'S A RELIEF.

THOUGHT YOU MIGHT HAVE DONATED IT TO OXFAM!
GOT TO FIND GABBY.

GOT TO...
NO.
NOT HERE...

Coming Soon:
The New
POWELL ESTATE
A Neon
Development
NO!
THE SCENARIOS HAVE TRIGGERED THE REQUIRED EMOTIONAL RESPONSE.
AND FROM THAT TURMOIL, WE HARVEST THE FUEL WE REQUIRE...

...SO THAT THE DOORS BETWEEN DIMENSIONS CAN BE ERODED...

...AND PURIFICATION CAN BEGIN!!!

FZZZK
WHAT'S UP, DOC?

GABBY?
HOW ARE YOU--?!

HARD TO EXPLAIN, BUT LET'S JUST SAY...

...SOME FAMILIAR FACES CAUGHT ME WHEN I FELL!
WE DON'T HAVE MUCH TIME THOUGH, DOCTOR.
THE REACH'S PLAN IS MORE SERIOUS THAN WE THOUGHT.
OH, UNDOUBTEDLY. FILL ME IN ON THE WAY---
"--WE HAVE WORLDS TO SAVE!"
FZZZK

THE DOORS ARE ALMOST OPEN!
SOON THE FEEDBACK WAVE WILL REACH ITS PEAK...

...AND MY GRASP W EXTEND ACR DIMENSION

FZZZK
SPOKE TOO SOON!

HOW... IS THIS POSSIBLE?
LOTS OF FANCY ANSWERS I COULD GIVE, BUT BASICALLY ...

...YOU HAVE *ENEMIES,* BUT WE HAVE *FRIENDS!*
NO.

I MEAN, IT WAS A GOOD PLAN.
YOUR OPLE -- THE OYS IN BLUE RE! -- EXILE OU, THEIR T DANGEROUS MINAL, INSIDE A POCKET UNIVERSE.
COSY, BUT THE WORST RISON I'VE SEEN.
"TIME PASSES AND YOU 'REACH' OUT, LOOKING FOR AN ESCAPE.
"AND, AS LUCK WOULD HAVE IT, YOU FIND ONE: A FISSURE IN TIME AND SPACE, LOCATED HERE IN LONDON AND THEN, USING YOUR LIMITED POWERS --
OU NAB YOURSELF SOME SPERATE LOCAL HELP!
"WITH CROSSLAND AS YOUR LINK TO THIS UNIVERSE, YOU TURNED YOUR SIGHTS ONTO YOUR REAL TARGET...
"... ME!
"OR RATHER... ALL MY LOSS... ALL OF MY RAGE AND PAIN ASSOCIATED WITH THIS CITY."

AND SOMEHOW YOU PLANNED TO SIPHON ALL THAT NERGY OFF INTO AN OTIONAL WMD YOU OULD POINT BACK AT OUR PEOPLE -- TO WIPE THEM FROM CREATION.
ANYTHING TO SAY FOR YOURSELF, SCARLET?

WHY USE WORDS?

AGGHHH!

DOCTOR... I DON'T THINK... I CAN...
NOR... CAN... I...

CROSSLAND... I KNOW YOU'RE STILL IN THERE! THE... FEEDBACK WAVE THE REACH WILL UNLEASH....
IT WON'T JUST WIPE HIS PEOPLE OUT... THE BLOWBACK WILL TAKE OUT HALF OF LONDON!
IS THAT WHAT YOU WANT?

I... I...
IGNORE HIM!

NO! HE REACHED YOU WHEN YOU WERE WEAK... BUT HE DOESN'T OWN YOUR SOUL!
FIGHT HIM!

I'M SORRY.

BUT THAT'S THE GOOD THING ABOUT DOORS.
ONCE OPENED...

...THEY CAN ALWAYS BE CLOSED!
NOOOOOOOOO!
SLAM
COME ON, RUN!

SFZZZZK
SFZZZZK

KABOOM

"WHEN CROSSLAND SEVERED THE REACH'S LINK TO THIS DIMENSION... THE FISSURE HE EXPLOITED WAS SEALED FOREVER."

WITH HIS DYING BREATH HE SAVED TWO WORLDS. ...WOULD THAT WE WERE ALL SO LUCKY.
POLICE BOX
SO... WHERE DO YOU FANCY GOING NEX--
HOW DO YOU DO IT?
I'M SORRY?

YOU WERE RIGHT: I DON'T KNOW YOU. NOT ALL OF YOU. AND I'VE MET MORE THAN ONE!
ALL THAT PAIN, RAGE AND ANGER... I'D NOT SEEN THAT BEFORE TODAY.

TODAY YOU WERE LUCKY, I CAME BACK.
...WHAT IF I HADN'T?

WHAT WOULD YOU HAVE DONE IF YOU'D LOST ME TOO?

HOW ABOUT A NIGHT AT THE LIGHT OPERA ON OLPHUS 9? OR A VISIT TO THE WIDE WING OF THE HIGH SHANSHEETH NEST?

GREAT BIG BIRDS IN FEATHER BOAS! IT'S LIKE GOING TO A HINGE AND BRACKET CONVENTION!
DO THOSE THINGS EVEN EXIST? I THINK WE NEED TO FIND OUT!
...
...WHATEVER YOU SAY, DOCTOR.

"WHATEVER YOU SAY."
VWOORRR
VWOORRR
THE END!

WELLINGTON
DIAZ
2016

POLI
BOX

DADDY'S HOME!

POLICE PUBLIC CALL BOX
POLICE PUBLIC CALL BOX

POLICE
PUBLIC CALL

FOLLOW YOUR FAVORITE INCARNATIONS ACROSS THESE FANTASTIC COLLECTIONS!

DOCTOR WHO: THE TWELFTH DOCTOR VOL. 1: TERRORFORMER

ISBN: 9781782761778
ON SALE NOW - $19.99 / $22.95 CAN / £10.99
(UK EDITION ISBN: 9781782763864)

DOCTOR WHO: THE TWELFTH DOCTOR VOL. 2: FRACTURES

ISBN: 9781782763017
ON SALE NOW - $19.99 / $25.99 CAN / £10.99
(UK EDITION ISBN: 9781782766599)

DOCTOR WHO: THE TWELFTH DOCTOR VOL. 3: HYPERION

ISBN: 9781782767473
ON SALE NOW- $19.99 / $25.99 CAN / £10.99
(UK EDITION ISBN: 97817827674442)

DOCTOR WHO: THE TWELFTH DOCTOR VOL. 4: THE SCHOOL OF DEATH

ISBN: 9781785851087
COMING SOON - $19.99 / $25.99 CAN / £10.99
(UK EDITION ISBN: 9781785851070)

DOCTOR WHO: THE ELEVENTH DOCTOR VOL. 1: AFTER LIFE

ISBN: 9781782761747
ON SALE NOW - $19.99 / $22.95 CAN / £10.99
(UK EDITION ISBN: 9781782763857)

DOCTOR WHO: THE ELEVENTH DOCTOR VOL. 2: SERVE YOU

ISBN: 9781782761754
ON SALE NOW - $19.99 / $25.99 CAN / £10.99
(UK EDITION ISBN: 9781782766582)

DOCTOR WHO: THE ELEVENTH DOCTOR VOL. 3: CONVERSION

ISBN: 9781782763024
ON SALE NOW - $19.99 / $25.99 CAN / £10.99
(UK EDITION ISBN: 9781782767435)

DOCTOR WHO: THE ELEVENTH DOCTOR VOL. 4: THE THEN AND THE NOW

ISBN: 9781782767466
ON SALE NOW - $19.99 / $25.99 CAN / £10.99
(UK EDITION ISBN: 9781722767428)

For information on how to subscribe to our great Doctor Who titles, or to purchase them digitally for your favorite device, visit:

WWW.TITAN-COMICS.COM

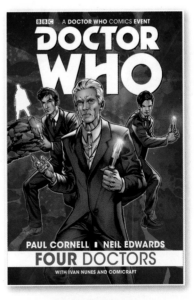

NO.
NO!
NOOOO!
VREEE
VZZBBBZZEEEE

BIOGRAPHIES

Nick Abadzis was born in Sweden to Greek and British parents and was brought up in England and Switzerland. He has been writing and drawing comics and graphic novels for over twenty-five years. His work has appeared in numerous books and periodicals around the world and he has been honored with various international storytelling awards, including an Eisner for his 2007 graphic novel, *Laika*. He lives in the USA with his wife and daughter.

James Peaty is a veteran comics writer, having worked for DC on *Supergirl* and *Justice League* and for Marvel on *X-Men Unlimited*.

Giorgia Sposito is an Italian artist and inker who has worked on many titles such as *Charmed* and *Wonderland*.

Warren Pleece is a British comics artist, famous for his work on *True Faith, The Invisibles* and *The Great Unwashed*.

Arianna Florean is a talented artist and cartoonist in her own right, and brings the Tenth Doctor to life with her beautiful coloring. She lives and works in Rome, Italy,

Hi-Fi is a digital color studio, founded by Brian and Kristy Miller in 1998. They have worked in comics, animation, and video games. Most recently, they have curated the *Femme Magnifique* anthology, celebrating inspirational women.